Confronting
Sexual Harassment:

Learning Activities
for Teens

by

Russell A. Sabella, Ph.D.

and

Robert D. Myrick, Ph.D.

Publisher—

Educational Media Corporation®
PO Box 21311
Minneapolis, MN 55421-0311

Production Editor—
Don L. Sorenson

Graphic Design—
Earl R. Sorenson

Russell A. Sabella, Ph.D. & Robert D. Myrick, Ph.D.

Dedication

To my parents, Giuseppe and Sina, for your love, dedication, and support. And to my wife, Betty, and son, Giuseppe, I appreciate and love you both so much.

RAS.

and

To Kaylen Myrick and to all of her friends.

RDM.

About the Authors

Russell A. Sabella, Ph.D. is a middle school counselor in Alachua County Schools, Gainesville, Florida. He has presented programs at state and national conferences for counselors and peer helper trainers on sexual assault, date rape, and sexual harassment. As a university counselor, he provided counseling and consultation services to victims of sexual abuse. As a high school teacher, he trained peer helpers to deliver developmental guidance units. As a dropout prevention counselor, he has provided individual counseling, small group counseling, and taught self-contained classes for at-risk students.

Robert D. Myrick is professor, Counselor Education, College of Education, University of Florida, Gainesville, Florida. He teaches courses in Counseling Children, Counseling Adolescents, and Play Counseling, among others, that focus on developmental guidance and counseling. He is recognized for his publications and workshops related to the training of trainers of peer facilitators and helpers, middle and high school teacher-advisor programs, and the preparation of school counselors and teachers.

Table of Contents

Dedication 3

About the Authors 4

Preface 7

Chapter 1 **Sexual Harassment: A Pervasive Problem** 9

Chapter 2 **Sexual Harassment: A Costly Problem** 19

The Cost to Business 20

The Cost to Educational Institutions 23

The Cost to Personal Development 25

Chapter 3 **Sexual Harassment: Confronting the Problem** 33

Sex Role Stereotypes 33

The Myths of Harassment 35

Chapter 4 **Sexual Harassment: Helping Resolve the Problem** 39

Four Personality Profiles 40

Related Issues 42

Caring People Can Help 44

Chapter 5 **Confronting Sexual Harassment: A Guidance Unit** 55

Working with Teenagers 56

Working with Parents 57

Figure 5.1: Sample Parent Permission Form 59

Summary of Sessions 60

Session 1: The Nature of the Beast 61

Activity 1.1: "Tic-Tac-Know!" 61

Session 2: Sexual Harassment Mythology 66

Activity 2.1: Go to Your Corner! 67

Session 3: Is it Sexual Harassment? 70

Activity 3.1: Is it Sexual Harassment? 70

Session 4: The Web 76

Activity 4.1: The Spider Web 76

Session 5: What are You Trying to Say? 79

Activity 5.1: You Gizzydeech! 80

Activity 5.2: The Blind Spot 82

Session 6: Hey! You're in My Space! 84

Activity 6.1: The Party 84

Session 7: Helping Yourself and Others 86

Activity 7.1: Opt to STOP! 87

Activity 7.2: Helping a Friend Who Has Been Sexually Harassed 88

Session 8: Moving Around and Moving Ahead 91

Activity 8.1: I Learned 91

Chapter 6 **Supplemental Activities** 93

Dear Abby 93

A Public Survey 95

Monkey See, Monkey Do 95

Try to Escape 96

Unfinished Sentences 96

The Dating Ritual 97

The Graffiti Wall 98

To Catch a Thief 99

Chapter 6   Supplemental Activites (continued)
Reporting a Murder 100
The Mystery Person 101
My Body 102
I Want You To... 102
The Nightly News 103
Enclosure 103
Complete the Sentences 104
Red Light, Green Light, Yellow Light 105
Debate 106
A Boy Who... (Rank Order) 107
Order in the Court 108
Masks 108
To Build a House of Cards 109
The Mannequins 110
Listen to the Music 110
What's Happening Here? 111
The Feedback Chair 111
Mobile 112
Crossword Puzzle 113

Chapter 7   The Facilitative Model and Group Leadership **117**
The Facilitative Conditions 118
The Facilitative Processes 121
The High Facilitative Responses 126
Figure 7.1 Feeling Words 128
The Low Facilitative Responses 133
Facilitative Responses in Conducting the Unit 139
The Facilitative Activities 141

Chapter 8   Accountability and Evaluation **143**
Figure 8.1 The Sexual Harassment Inventory 145
Figure 8.2 The School Atmosphere Inventory 147
Figure 8.3 Sexual Harassment Unit Evaluation 148
Scoring and Interpretation 149
What Students Think of the Unit 150

Session Reproducibles **153**
Session 1: Reproducibles 154
Session 2: Reproducibles 156
Session 3: Reproducibles 161
Session 5: Reproducibles 164
Session 6: Reproducibles 166
Session 7: Reproducibles 170
Session 8: Reproducibles 173

References and Related Readings **175**

Russell A. Sabella, Ph.D. & Robert D. Myrick, Ph.D.

Preface

Every generation grows up in a different world than their parents. Today's children are the first daycare generation, the first to grow up in an electronic society full of computers and surrounded by new forms of multimedia technology. They live in a world of abstraction more than reality, as environment and nature become more of a projected image than something experienced first hand. They are the first post-sexual revolution generation, being exposed to more sexually explicit pictures and language on television and films. The children of today have more options; but, overloaded with choices, they may not always make responsible decisions and act appropriately, especially in terms of social relationships.

Parents and family members, ideally, should have enough time together to talk about life's issues, including how to relate with others and to create satisfying personal relationships. However, it is well-documented that many children in this generation are being raised in single-parent families, often with a working mother who is lucky to have time and energy left for quality family time. Traditional families, where the teaching of social values and customs was once lodged, are giving way to new family structures and new childhood freedoms that did not exist forty years ago.

To create a safe and productive society, caring adults must help children address some of the issues that are influencing their development and the world they will live in. This can be challenging, for adults often project their own fears and wishes on young people. Older generations typically rely on their own experiences as primary reference points to make decisions and give direction to children. Sometimes this can be effective and at other times it is risky, if not detrimental.

For example, there were many generations of men and women who learned that it was useless to challenge someone who harassed them. Sexual harassment of women was considered part of life's game, a playful battle between the sexes. Women, especially, were taught to tolerate it, to ignore the humiliation, and that it was probably best not to say anything. To speak up would only fuel the situation and possibly make matters worse.

But, times have changed. Sexual harassment is no longer tolerated. A new generation of children are being taught they need not sacrifice their dignity and personal welfare as either the butt of insensitive jokes or through intimidating sexual threats.

This book is about sexual harassment. It is designed to help caring adults—teachers, counselors, and others—work with young people regarding the development of positive personal relationships. More specifically, it is an attempt to address the particularly troublesome area of harassment. It includes some general information and background which highlight the problem and provides a rationale for the guidance unit that follows.

The guidance unit is entitled "Confronting Sexual Harassment." Aimed at middle and high school students, it consists of eight group sessions, each with objectives, procedures, and activities. Students learn concepts and skills as they progress through the unit. They are challenged to take more responsibility in creating a safe and productive school environment.

The unit was designed to stand alone or to be integrated into the curricula of regular middle or high school courses. Teachers, for example, might use the unit as a departure point to also teach writing and speaking skills in English classes, or as part of human development in science. Counselors might want to present the unit in their work, either meeting with classroom groups or perhaps as a small group counseling unit with selected students. The unit can also be used in other settings, such as mental health agencies, religious centers, and community organizations.

The guidance unit was originally viewed as one with twelve sessions; however, it was decided to present and test a time-limited model. Supplemental activities are included for those who have more time and access to young people who would volunteer to participate in the experience.

Some assessment instruments are also included. These can be used as an individual or group pre-post measure of concepts and skills. We are indebted to the students and teachers who helped us develop and test the unit. There are too many to be named here. However, particular appreciation goes to the counselors, teachers, and students of Ft. Clark Middle School, Westwood Middle School, and the Teen Aiders of Buchholz High School, all in the Alachua County Schools, Gainesville, Florida. Counselor education students at the University of Florida deserve special thanks for their insights and help piloting the program.

The authors recognize that the topic of sexual harassment is sensitive and sometimes controversial. The problems involved can take the form of many different behaviors and also vary across situations. This book is aimed at the general population of teenagers and the most typical situations. These can be adapted to special situations not covered here.

Also, we were sensitive to the use of pronouns and how they might convey a message about one particular gender or the other. By no means are all males guilty of sexual harassment, just as all females are not victims. We also recognize that, while our examples may depict people of the opposite gender, sexual harassment also occurs between people of the same gender and, in fewer than ten percent of all cases, a female can also be guilty of sexually harassing a male.

Finally, special thanks go to Betty Sabella and Linda Myrick who helped critique the manuscript, sharpened the focus of the unit, and offered their continuing support.

Russell A. Sabella
Robert D. Myrick
May, 1995

Sexual Harassment: A Pervasive Problem

A child is born and immediately labeled as either a boy or a girl. From that time on, he or she will be raised somewhat differently, each learning the gender roles and behaviors established by their respective families and communities. But, it is not an easy learning experience, as many people are mystified and confused by their sexual feelings.

Sex is a powerful life force and influences everyone's personal development and lifestyle. It brings joy and it also brings problems. It entails much more than biological reproduction, with profound implications on the psychological and sociological aspects of human beings and their daily lives. Religious leaders, scholars, legislators, and judges throughout history have attempted to define and clarify the nature and responsibility of interpersonal and sexual relationships.

Sex is a powerful life force....

Since the 1950s sex has been talked about more openly. Sex is a natural part of life and nothing about which to be ashamed. Because it involves deep personal feelings and desires, however, it has not always been an easy topic to discuss rationally.

Many people still blush, giggle, and quickly dismiss the subject of sex out of embarrassment. In other situations, people treat sex as obscene and tell "dirty jokes" using sexual language and encounters, hoping to amuse others. In some cases, the topic makes individuals feel so inadequate and uncertain about themselves that they are unable to form effective interpersonal relationships. In far too many situations, misconceptions and misunderstandings about sex have led to personal and social problems that are detrimental not only to individuals but to society.

One of the related troublesome areas in our nation is sexual harassment. While the problem has its origins in human sexuality, it is also rooted in the lack of respect and acceptance of people. It has become an undignified and pervasive problem that can no longer be tolerated.

Harmless Teasing or Harassment?

Flirting is considered an act of playful love. It's positive, may be frivolous, and often is an attempt to engage someone in a light-hearted exchange that communicates positive attraction. In this case, those involved feel special, complimented, valued, and perhaps intrigued. They may even feel flattered and revered; there is reciprocal or mutual understanding; the teasing and flirting is mutually experienced as fun.

When similar words and actions are not perceived as playful flirting, then continued exchanges might become hurtful. In this case, actions may be demeaning, humiliating, embarrassing, and certainly unwanted.

Lawrence Kutner, a syndicated columnist, described an incident that captured people's attention. It started on a school bus when a tenth grade girl with red hair was called "Fire Crotch" by several sixth grade boys, who giggled and snickered among themselves.

...no fun in being dishonored and humiliated.

"I was embarrassed," said Millie, who asked that her last name and town not be used in order to avoid further harassment. "I told them not to say it, but they kept on. Then, I tried to ignore them." Her sister overheard the comments and complained to the bus driver, the school principal, and a teacher—all of whom said that nothing much could be done. Millie's mother spoke to the principal and the bus company.

For several months nothing changed, until the mother started using the term "sexual harassment" in her conversations with officials. Action was then taken. The boys were assigned seats behind the driver and were told that if name-calling continued, they would not be allowed to ride the bus.

Sexual harassment of children by children is a difficult topic since playful teasing is often a part of childhood experiences. When is it harmless? When is teasing no longer playful but hurtful? When does it go beyond youthful exuberance?

Sexual harassment can take place in homes, schools, places of business, in shopping malls, or on the streets. It is intended to put another person down through humiliation and dominance. In some cases, sexual harassment is thought to maintain the status quo of male dominance and power in the workplace.

Russell A. Sabella, Ph.D. & Robert D. Myrick, Ph.D.

"Aw, come on, can't you take a joke? Where's your sense of fun? Loosen up and don't be so uptight." These and similar statements typically follow sexually harassing comments that have gone beyond the confines of teasing and good humor. Rather, the comments were degrading and caused embarrassment. There is no fun in being dishonored and humiliated.

...in every community there are always inappropriate behaviors being modeled for children.

Some harassers have claimed their innocence by saying, "I didn't know." But, ignorance is neither an excuse for disrespect nor a right to demean and hurt the feelings of others. There are, no doubt, cases when people are simply copying or imitating an insulting behavior without much awareness of what they are doing. Patterns of interaction with people are often learned by observing others and then repeating or mimicking their behaviors, especially those behaviors that show or demonstrate a sense of power. Unfortunately, in every community there are always inappropriate behaviors being modeled for children.

The jump from teasing to harassment is not always obvious to people. This rings true especially when the victim is male. Michael Crichton's novel, *Disclosure,* depicted a case involving a man who was accused of sexual harassment by his female boss. Once he shockingly discovered the claim, he immediately maintained that it was he that was actually the victim of sexual harassment and not her. A central question permeated throughout was, "Who has the power?" The answer was not always apparent or clear.

Further, Crichton's (1993) book depicted the emotional turmoil, humiliation, and damage to the man's family and career. Even though he was vindicated, it is highly illustrative of how sexual harassment can hurt anyone, regardless of gender, age, race, or religion. The difference in status or power of the abuser over the victim—a hallmark of sexual harassment in the workplace—is not as apparent with children or young people either. But, it is there.

What Is Sexual Harassment?

In the simplest of words, sexual harassment is any unwelcome sexual advance, request for sexual favors, or other forms of verbal or physical conduct of a sexual nature. "Unwelcome" is the key word.

If a sexually suggestive statement is made in earnest or in jest, it is not sexual harassment if the recipient is not offended or doesn't care. Some people may even join in sexual banter, feeling no hurt or embarrassment, and overlook the behavior. It is seen as reproachable but blameless. On the other hand, when something is done that is disconcerting and upsetting to an individual, then matters have gone too far and teasing has turned to taunting. The offended person feels abused and insulted. Any behavior that elicits this kind of response is insensitive and unwelcome. It is unacceptable and may even be criminal.

The idea of consent is what makes sexual harassment difficult to define, learn, and prevent. It is the source of much debate, tension, and frustration. The range of offensiveness among individuals can span great lengths. What is clearly offensive to one person may not be offensive at all to another. Although it may not be appropriate, sexual language used in a place such as the school environment may not necessarily constitute sexual harassment.

Would you hide what you said from your mother?

In addition to consent, the element of repetitiveness is usually considered when trying to establish whether sexual harassment has taken place. One incident of unwanted sexual attention may not be the same as recurring incidents, especially after the perpetrator is confronted. At first, the victim may not feel harassed but annoyed or irritated. Eventually, this may change into feelings that constitute harassment such as fear, powerlessness, and helplessness.

Bernice Sandler, a senior associate with the Center for Women Policy Studies in Washington, D.C., suggested three questions people can ask themselves to determine if something they say or might say could be a form of sexual harassment. It is probably a form of sexual harassment if you answer "yes" to any of the following questions: Would you hide what you said from your mother? Would you mind if someone said the same thing to your sisters? Would you be embarrassed if you were quoted in the newspaper?

Russell A. Sabella, Ph.D. & Robert D. Myrick, Ph.D.

The Harassed and the Harassers

The primary consideration which compels sexual harassment intervention efforts is the experience of the victim. The distress a victim may endure can have far reaching repercussions. Experiencing violence can change the way a person sees himself or herself. Often times their identity can change from student or child to victim. It is unlikely that once victimized, at the very least, he or she can never again feel quite as safe or secure.

Although there may be distinctions among events, a remarkably consistent picture of the mental health impact of violence on victims emerges from the empirical and clinical literature. A victim may experience a post traumatic stress disorder which may include:

- depression
- denial
- disturbances of self-esteem
- emotional numbness
- fear/avoidance
- food/drug/alcohol abuse
- hyperalertness
- hypersexuality
- low self-confidence
- migraines
- muscle spasms
- paranoia
- sexual dysfunction
- suppression
- tension
- other medical illnesses

Sexual harassers... are usually people with a "hangup" about power....

Sexual harassers are known to have several general characteristics which incorporate a profile. They are usually people with a "hangup" about power and are considered bullies. They like to give orders and make other people afraid. Harassers are often people who will do anything to have their own way. They often pick up the wrong message from television and movies about what other people want. A harasser can be sadistic, someone who simply enjoys inflicting pain in others (Bouchard, 1990).

Three Kinds of Sexual Harassment

If sexual harassment is unwelcome sexually suggestive behavior and we want to prevent it from happening, we need to know that it may appear in different forms. In general, three kinds of sexual harassment have been identified: physical harassment, visual harassment, and verbal harassment. All of these have taken place in schools and workplaces, as well as homes and neighborhoods.

Physical harassment is an unwelcome contact such as bumping, touching, hugging, kissing, groping, or pinching. Where it takes place has no bearing on the matter. It is a case of physical space, especially private body parts, being intruded upon by another.

Visual harassment is unwelcome exposure to sexually explicit photos, drawings, cartoons, notes, magazines, posters, graffiti, and staring. It might be in the form of a glossy picture used as a pin-up or in a hastily scribbled note with words or pictures that are sexually suggestive.

Verbal harassment consists of unwelcome spoken words or sounds directed toward another, such as lewd or suggestive remarks, off-colored jokes, wolf whistles, or comments on a person's appearance. Unwelcome invitations for a date or sexual relations, especially those that are repeated after being denied, are also included.

...people may experience sexual harassment even if the behavior or material is not directly focused on them.

Physical, visual, and verbal sexual harassment may be directly focused on an individual. However, people may experience sexual harassment even if the behavior or material is not directly focused on them. A person can become the victim of sexual harassment when the action of others creates a hostile working environment. For example, a student sits between two others who continually make suggestive faces at each other or tell jokes of a sexual nature. If the middle student is offended, then he or she is said to have been subjected to a hostile working environment. This can be just as personally harmful and debilitating as sexual harassment directly targeted to any one person.

Quid Pro Quo threats (literally meaning "this for that") occur when individuals face harmful consequences (e.g., a lower grade or exclusion from an organization such as the band) if they don't give in to the demands of the authority figure (e.g., teacher or administrator) or, when applicable, other students. The demand may be a sexual favor or that someone tolerate a hostile working environment.

Russell A. Sabella, Ph.D. & Robert D. Myrick, Ph.D.

Sexual Harassment in the Workplace

Sexual harassment has been an element of American society for decades. In the workplace, it has been of great concern to many people. A hostile working environment exists when harassment is severe or pervasive enough that it affects a worker's ability to perform (e.g., attend work, participate in meetings and projects, and concentrate on production tasks).

It has resulted in court cases that, in turn, have led to judicial rulings focusing attention on the nature and problem of harassment. The legal basis of sexual harassment is found in Title VII, Civil Rights Act of 1964:

It shall be an unlawful employment practice for an employer: (1) to fail or refuse to hire or to discharge any individual, or otherwise to discriminate against any individual with respect to his [or her] compensation, terms, conditions, or privileges of employment because of such individual's race, color, religion, sex, or national origin or (2) to limit, segregate, or classify his [or her] employees or applicants for employment in any way which would deprive or tend to deprive any individual of employment opportunities or otherwise adversely affect his [or her] status as an employee, because of such individual's race, color, religion, sex, or national origin.

Prior to the 1980s, there were no federal or state laws prohibiting sexual harassment on the job....

Prior to the 1980s, there were no federal or state laws prohibiting sexual harassment on the job and few instances in which it was prevented or punished. A woman who was beaten, molested, or raped in the work place might file an assault or battery lawsuit, for example, but that happened rarely. The term sexual harassment was not known (Petrocelli & Repa, 1992). In 1986 the Supreme Court further defined two forms of sexual harassment previously described: Hostile Environment and Quid Pro Quo.

Sexual Harassment in the Schools

...four out of five teenagers have experienced some form of sexual harassment at school.

Sexual harassment is recognized as being widespread in our public schools. For instance, a recent study commissioned by the American Association of University Women (AAUW) Educational Foundation and conducted by Louis Harris and Associates, questioned 1,600 public school students in grades eight through twelve from 79 schools across the United States. The survey showed that four out of five teenagers have experienced some form of sexual harassment at school. Further, one in ten said they had been forced to commit a sexual act, beyond kissing, during school hours. And while most of the harassing came from schoolmates, one-fourth of the girls and one-tenth of the boys said they had been harassed by school employees (Harris, 1993).

The survey employed a broad definition of sexual harassment, including sexual comments or jokes; spreading sexual rumors about another student; touching, grabbing, or pinching in a sexual way; spying on a student who was dressing or showering; pulling another student's clothing off; forcing a kiss; "mooning" another student; or forcing another student to "do something sexual, other than kissing."

Sexual harassment, which takes place in almost every school, is a growing problem. The following statistics reflect the extent of the problem (Harris, 1993):

- Four of five students (about 81%) said they have experienced some form of sexual harassment during their school lives; 85% of girls and 76% of boys.
- One of three students (32%) who have been harassed first experienced sexual harassment in grade six or earlier.
- Two of three of all students who were surveyed (66%) have been targets of sexual comments, jokes, looks and gestures as well as touching, grabbing, and/or pinching in a sexual way.
- Nearly four of five students (79%) who have been harassed have been targeted by peers—current or former students. Eighteen percent (18%) of students who have been harassed cited adults as the perpetrators.
- Two of three students who have been harassed (66%) said they have been harassed in the hallway.

Sexual harassment could be the beginning of more intense forms of sexual misconduct. The following gives a "picture" of the problem with sexual assault:

Russell A. Sabella, Ph.D. & Robert D. Myrick, Ph.D.

- 25% of college women will experience being victimized by an attempted or completed rape, and one in three women will be the victim of some type of sexual assault in her life-time. This means that, statistically speaking, in a classroom with 16 women, four will become victims.

- 10% of reported rapes happen to men; 98% of the time the rapist is a man.

- 25% of college men reported using violence or threats of violence to force sexual relations.

- About 33% of college men surveyed reported they would rape a woman if they knew they would get away with it.

- Between five and 15% of college men repeatedly engage in behaviors legally considered to be rape; as many as 85% of college males have engaged in rape related behaviors at some time.

- In college rapes, the male was drinking alcohol or using drugs 75% of the time, the female was drinking or using drugs 57% of the time.

- Most rape victims and rapists are between the ages of 15 and 24. The median age for the victim is 18.

Although the majority of people who are victims of sexual harassment are female... males have also been harassed....

Although the majority of people who are victims of sexual harassment are female, there are situations where males have also been harassed—by females and other males. As society has changed, people have become freer to express themselves. Once restricted by traditional concepts, boys and girls (also men and women) have more freedom to enjoy one another. However, with freedom comes responsibility, and only an irresponsible person engages in sexual harassment.

Anthony was a popular boy at his school. Only in the tenth grade, he was the student body vice president and on the basketball team. Several girls were constantly asking him for a date and some said they wanted to go steady with him.

One girl, Diana, was adamant about becoming his girlfriend. She persistently left him notes, had her own friends approach him about it, and called him on the phone. After some time, she began to feel rejected, angry, and embarrassed. She began making comments like, "What's wrong with you? Are you gay or something?" and, "You don't know what your missing, probably you wouldn't know what to do anyway!" Diana then began making comments more sexual in nature and much more intense. Anthony didn't know what to do. He felt too embarrassed to say anything. He began to wonder if there was something wrong with him. He wondered what he did to deserve such treatment.

As in Anthony's case, and others, the issue of harassment goes beyond plain sexual meanings or requests. Rather, the suggestive actions are expressions of power, aggression, and dominance.

The Schools and the Courts

...students who are victims of sexual harassment can pursue monetary damages from their schools....

The United States Supreme Court unanimously ruled that students who are victims of sexual harassment can pursue monetary damages from their schools and school officials for violating their civil rights. The most highly acclaimed Supreme Court Case regarding sexual harassment in the schools is that of Franklin v. Gwinnett County Public Schools (No. 90-918) decided in February of 1992. Christine Franklin, a student in a high school filed an action for damages under Title IX of the Education Amendments of 1972 alleging that a teacher sexually harassed and abused her. It was held that damages remedy is available for an action brought to enforce Title IX.

Although the majority of sexual harassment claims are brought by women employees in the world of work, it is evident that the problem begins in neighborhoods, playgrounds, and schools where children and teenagers interact. And, schools are now being held more responsible for maintaining a safe and friendly learning environment that is free from sexual harassment. Schools are the workplace of students.

Sexual Harassment: A Costly Problem

Sexual harassment has become a costly problem to society. More specifically, businesses, schools, and personal development suffer when people fail to treat one another with kindness and mutual respect. An economic and personal loss is reflected in the form of work products, student achievement, career advancement, and monetary damages.

Some people may see a new guidance program as costly in terms of time, energy, and a commitment of resources. Teachers and parents, for example, may view additional developmental units directed to all students as a costly investment of school resources and classroom time. Many teachers are protective of their time with students and a few might questions the value of implementing a unit on sexual harassment during the school day.

However, time invested not only brings positive returns through improved working relationships in the school, but it can also avoid time-consuming conflicts, discipline referrals, and costly litigation. Sexual harassment is costly.

The Cost to Business

Courtesy and the Courts

When common courtesies are not extended to people, problems occur in working relationships and productivity suffers. In both school and business, sexual harassment and the lack of common courtesy have led to disagreements. The cost to Corporate America to settle future law suits related to sexual harassment has been estimated at eleven billion dollars over the next five years. In many cases, significant financial judgments have been made already. Consider the following cases in point that came from an electronic search (LEXIS/NEXIS database, 1994) of all major business journals:

- A board of inquiry appointed under the Ontario Human Rights Code ordered a Toronto employer to pay $31,000 to two women who were sexually harassed on the job. Their employer swore at the women, grabbed them, tried several times to kiss them, and repeatedly asked them about their private love lives (January 6, 1994).

- The State of Michigan decided to drop further appeals and to pay a $1 million judgment in a Lansing sexual harassment case. The president of a women's advocacy group called WINGS (Women Involved in Giving Support) stated that, "It should serve as a million-dollar message to employers and supervisors that sexual harassment can be very expensive and harassers are going to pay for their behavior" (October 18, 1994).

- According to a recent two-year U.S. study, sexual harassment of its employees cost the federal government an estimated $267 million—showing an astronomical $80 million increase in just five years over a previous similar study (July 21, 1992).

- The New York Supreme Court awarded $38,000 to a 37-year-old woman because of the sexual harassment she experienced at a company picnic (June 6, 1991).

- A South Florida firm was ordered to pay a college intern $1.3 million after she proved she was sexually harassed on the job (August 29, 1992).

- A typical Fortune 500 company loses $6.7 million a year due to absenteeism, turnover, and lost productivity caused by sexual harassment. Sexual harassment training in Fortune 500 companies has increased 35 percent since 1988. By 1992, 81 percent of these companies provided employees with sexual harassment training (October 12, 1992).

Sexual harassment can have a cumulative, demoralizing effect that discourages women from asserting themselves....

A company's image and reputation is an important part of its success. Advertising executives and public relations personnel devote substantial time and money towards getting consumers to experience trust, devotion, and confidence. Sexual harassment can jeopardize or destroy those feelings. Business relationships can deteriorate and profits can fall. With the popularity of the "superinformation highway" comes increased proliferation of information across millions of computers. Information regarding an incident of sexual harassment can potentially spread in a matter of minutes, altering perceptions about a company that may well be irreparable.

According to Petrocelli & Repa (1992), the consequences to working women as a group are no less serious. Sexual harassment can have a cumulative, demoralizing effect that discourages women from asserting themselves within the workplace, while among some men it reinforces stereotypes of women employees as sex objects.

For the individual in a company, sexual harassment can mean risk of losing one's job or chance of promotion. In other situations, unwelcome sexual actions can contribute to a hostile working environment which can in turn place pressure to leave a job. In some cases, related stresses can exhaust motivation, energy, enthusiasm, creativity, and support among co-workers.

The Massachusetts Supreme Court heard a case where a man had cut out a photograph of a 61-year-old woman who was running for president of her labor union where they both worked. He glued her head to the body of a naked model. What must he have been thinking as he circulated his artwork? How did others react? Although it may have been amusing to some, it infuriated the woman who decided to file a legal claim.

One of the issues in this case was that public figures are open to satire and people have the right to say whatever they like about them. But in January, 1995, the Massachusetts Supreme Court ruled that she had been attacked as a woman, not as a public figure open to ridicule and parody. This attack destroyed her ability to work with colleagues and created a sexually offensive environment. It was a case of harassment. Even if the woman decided to stay, chances were good that such an environment would have diminished her performance and productivity.

Tailhook: A Party That Crashed

Women have always played an important role in the military services. The notion of placing them in combat situations has generated a great deal of debate throughout the nation. As one woman said, "The truth is that most combat jobs in our high tech military no longer require brute strength." In most cases, an agile mind, quick reflexes, and cool courage are required. Those qualities, of course, are free of gender and there seems too few valid reasons for discriminating against women who want to be placed in combat-related jobs.

"This is not a joking matter," said one woman, "but, it seems that combat is related more to fighting off sexual advances than to engaging in armed combat with our nation's enemies." Too many women who are serving their country in the military services are being sexually harassed and even sexually assaulted.

In 1991 a national episode involving the United States Navy resulted in the disgrace of servicemen and their officers. The Navy was forced to reform its policies and procedures after some of its aviators held a convention that became synonymous with sexual harassment and assault (Tailhook). Women were called names, undressed, groped, and some were forced to run a gauntlet of men in a hotel hallway who fondled them as they ran by. These and other incidents led the Navy's Chief of Staff to reprimand several officers and to proclaim that sexual harassment would not be tolerated.

Sexual harassment threatened the honor and the effectiveness of the armed services....

The Navy first put women on noncombatant ships in 1978, and they now serve on 57 ships which train, fuel, supply and maintain the 406-ship fleet. In addition, nine combat ships, including the aircraft carrier Eisenhower, have women on board who play important roles in their crews. With 500,000 people in uniform, there would likely be some individuals who get out of line. Sexual harassment threatened the honor and the effectiveness of the armed services and this, above all else, would not be tolerated. The Navy was determined to be more vigilant and to punish offenders. Subsequently, educational programs were developed and presented at naval bases throughout the world.

It is essential to have women represented in the military. They have a long history of outstanding contributions in a variety of combat and noncombat roles. Our national security is threatened when sex-related problems hinder both the recruitment and the effectiveness of women and men in our military services. Sexual harassment cannot be tolerated and its prevention must be a part of early education.

The Cost to Educational Institutions

The loss of reputation, morale, and productivity due to sexual harassment is also true for schools, faculties, and students. The cost of sexual harassment to educational institutions is growing and must be confronted.

In Minnesota, a boy in the third grade was being taunted by classmates who used sexually explicit references. This harassment continued until his parents took him out of school during the fourth grade. They complained to school authorities who, at first, denied that the taunting constituted sexual harassment since there was no indication that the boy had been singled out for harassment because of his sex. The family appealed for help from state officials. This led to a ruling by the Department of Human Resources that the school district "did not take prompt and appropriate action... to stop the sexually harassing behavior" that was directed at the boy for nearly two years. State and district officials are negotiating a settlement.

...many school districts are being challenged and new directives are being issued.

Reasonable interpretations of guidelines and laws that might have made sense a few years ago in many school districts are being challenged and new directives are being issued. There is more legal support to permit investigations of sexual harassment issues and there is an increase in financial judgments against organizations and school districts in favor of those being harassed.

Consider the following cases:

- A high school girl filed suit against her school after officials did nothing about removing graffiti in the boy's bathroom that called her a "slut" and depicted her as doing demeaning acts with boys and animals. She made requests over 10 months to have the graffiti removed and for a long time didn't mention it to her parents. The student won a $15,000 settlement.

- A Texas civil rights group filed a federal lawsuit seeking $850,000 against a school district, alleging school leaders failed to protect two teenage girls from sexual harassment by three boys.

- In California, the U.S. Department of Education's Office of Civil Rights found that one school system failed to protect an eighth grade girl who repeatedly endured classmates' shouts of "moo, moo" and other taunts about her body. Her parents filed a lawsuit and settled out of court for $20,000.

- School officials in one Minnesota high school ignored a girl's complaints of vulgar treatment by boys for a year and a half until she filed charges with the state and won a $15,000 "mental anguish" settlement.

- Another Minnesota student, seven years old, became the first elementary school student in the nation to accuse her peers of sexual harassment. The student's mother filed a sex discrimination complaint against the school district charging that it failed to discourage harassment of her daughter and other girls who were subjected to nasty language, taunting, and other threats. In the settlement, the district agreed to institute a sexual harassment policy.

When students are the target of sexual harassment, their right to an equal education is compromised. Experiencing sexual harassment can interfere with learning, attendance, course choices, grades, and ultimately, economic outlook.

Consider that 23% of students who have been sexually harassed said that one outcome of the experience is not wanting to attend school. Nearly one in four girls said that harassment caused them to stay home from school or not attend a class. Since school attendance is directly related to performance, increased truancy can increase the risk of jeopardizing students' career potential.

Further, 23% of those experiencing sexual harassment reported not wanting to talk as much in class after experiencing sexual harassment (Harris, 1993). Several studies indicated there already exists a lower rate of class participation among female students as compared to male students at the elementary level (e.g., Biraimah, 1989; DeVoe, 1991; Visser, 1987). Experiencing sexual harassment can only add to the problem.

Twenty-one percent of students who have been sexually harassed said the experience made it more difficult to pay attention in school....

Twenty-one percent of students who have been sexually harassed said the experience made it more difficult to pay attention in school, sixteen percent of students said they have made a lower grade on a test or paper, thirteen percent made a lower grade in class, sixteen percent found it hard to study, twelve percent of the students who have been harassed had thoughts about changing schools, and a small percentage of students changed schools and doubted whether they had what it takes to graduate from high school because of sexual harassment (Harris, 1993).

School systems are limited in funds and resources and these need to be used in the education of young people. To drain these resources and tax dollars on legal fees and payment for personal damages is indefensible, especially in terms of cases involving sexual harassment.

The Cost to Personal Development

Self-esteem and self-confidence play an important role in learning and achieving. Students who feel good about themselves and who experience positive relationships tend to perform well. They achieve more and enjoy going to school. They see school as a friendly place to be. They form positive relationships with classmates and teachers which eventually carry into adulthood. However, sexual harassment can be costly to personal development.

Sticks and Stones

Sticks and stones may break your bones, but words can be just as hurtful....

Remember the old rhyme, "Sticks and stones may break my bones, but words can never hurt me?" It was seen as a quick and clever response to childhood taunts. Do you remember being mocked or scorned by other children when you were growing up? Maybe you recall a time when you saw someone else being insulted or ridiculed. Name-calling is so prevalent among children that it is rare to find someone who has never been verbally abused.

Even in childhood, verbal abusers gain some kind of satisfaction in using sarcasm or impolite words. Their words are weapons used to make a statement. The intended effect is to say, "I'm bigger and stronger than you," or, "I'm smarter and quicker than you, or perhaps, "You are not as important as I am." The message is: "I'm better, more powerful, and deserving than you."

Abusive words hurt. They create degrading pictures of people. They may not break bones but they can break one's spirit, at least for awhile. They often shape lasting perceptions and self-images. Do you remember a time when you were young and someone called you a name or said something abusive to you? It may have been another child or even an adult. Think back to one of those times.

The scene may still burn deep in your memory and the words may still make you flinch. You might vividly recall the event, the people involved, and remember the hurt. Or, you may not recall everything, but you remember the words and their impact on you. It matters not what you did in response, the simple fact is you remember and will carry the experience with you all of your life. Sticks and stones may break your bones, but words can be just as hurtful and also leave scars.

Counselors and teachers of children try to stop verbal abusiveness when they hear it. They assume that abusers are trying to bring attention to themselves, seeking revenge, or trying to demonstrate power. Such misbehavior, of course, is reprimanded; but it may continue out of the presence of critical adults.

Some authors (Collins & Collins, 1975; Thompson & Rudolph, 1983) have suggested hurtful teasing is a form of attention getting with several possible motives. What's the motivation? What do people gain from it? Is it to seek attention or to gain a sense of power? Is it a way of compensating for feelings of inadequacy or perhaps a means of covering up a learning or emotional problem? Could it be a case in which there is a lack of social skills and understanding of others? In addition, it's possible that hurtful teasing may have been modeled for abusers by people they admire in their family, community, or perhaps in a movie or television program. Regardless of the motive or where the behavior was learned, it can be reinforced when it hits its mark and results in personal satisfaction.

All elementary schools include the teaching of social skills in their curricula. Classroom discussions about unacceptable behaviors, role-playing and role-reversals, the isolation of offenders, and inclusion activities that help children learn to know and appreciate one another are common interventions most children experience in their classrooms.

One of the standard counseling techniques recommended to help victims of abusive language is to meet with them and explain if they do not respond to the words, it is not as satisfying to the abuser and the behavior will decrease. This makes common sense and often works. However, sexual harassment is so pervasive in society that it can no longer be ignored. It cannot be assumed that a few classroom discussions in the elementary school will suffice in confronting the problem sexual harassment.

It cannot be assumed that a few classroom discussions in the elementary school will suffice in confronting the problem sexual harassment.

When young people become teenagers, teasing takes on an additional meaning. Still an attention seeking behavior, it can be an attempt to be playful, or perhaps reach out to friends in a lighthearted way. Teasing is almost a ritual among close friends. In some cases, friendship may be defined by the ability to take part in private jests, inside jokes, and the use of intimate terms and expressions. The assumption is that true friends and close companions can play pranks on one another or make insulting taunts but still remain friends. It is all done in the sense of fun and comradeship.

Playful teasing has also been a traditional part of how boys and girls reach out and relate to one another. Many close relationships have developed from an amusing remark or observation. The comments may have been meant to respectfully gain attention and to enter the time and space of another person. These comments, however, were in all likelihood not intended to be hurtful, degrading, or humiliating. The impact of behavior on a person's feelings is the critical difference between light- hearted words and those that break the boundaries of kindness and respect.

Russell A. Sabella, Ph.D. & Robert D. Myrick, Ph.D.

Sexual banter among adults is socially acceptable in most close circles. Whether it is judged as having any socially redeeming value is questionable, but as long as it does not offend or hurt someone's feelings or reputation, it is allowed or tolerated. The problem is that even adults are not always open and honest about what they experience in such situations. Some may be offended and choose not to participate, to simply listen and tolerate or endure it. Ironically, childhood teachings suggest they first ignore it. This silent response often has a reinforcing effect and those initiating the suggestive jests or coarse humor may interpret the non-action as acceptance and even encouragement to repeat the same kind of behavior at another time.

As young people grow older and develop sexually, they are more at-risk of being abused.

One woman who was interviewed said that it was "about time" something was being done about the sexual abuses women have endured over the years. For too long it has been one of society's "dirty little secrets." She went on to say:

When I was younger I had a summer a job where almost every day I fought off the sexual advances of the manager. I was 17, naive, and scared. I wondered if I had done anything to entice him. I felt totally alone. I had no idea other women had similar experiences. I felt powerless. I needed the job, so I kept the secret to myself and was relieved beyond words when the summer ended.

As young people grow older and develop sexually, they are more at-risk of being abused. Because of their maturing bodies, they can be seen as sexual objects by others, who are only attuned to physical appearances. Some encounter sexual innuendo and related experiences that they might initially enjoy because it makes them feel noticed and grown-up. Others are embarrassed and flustered by anything that draws attention to bodily changes and the possible sexual implications of such transformations.

As children become teenagers, they need an opportunity to talk about their changing bodies and what it means in terms of social conduct. They are no longer little children watching and learning about body parts in an elementary school "human development" unit. The transition from childhood to young men and women is in progress and cannot be stopped. Sexuality now has more personal meaning as puberty increases their interest in sexual matters. What teenagers learn about themselves and others is important to both the welfare of themselves and society.

Personal and School Achievement

Students who experience sexual harassment do not want to go to school. Or, if they do, they worry throughout the day that they are going to be teased and insulted. They may avoid going to a certain area of the school, even though it means missing or being tardy to a class. While in a classroom with harassers, a person may choose to remain silent and not participate fully in class activities in an attempt not to draw attention.

These students are often preoccupied with their helplessness and how to avoid creating a scene. It's hard for them to concentrate and complete school tasks. They often avoid eye contact and turn down opportunities to speak in front of a class. They are self-conscious and defensive. All of this detracts from their ability to apply themselves to school assignments. Achievement becomes more difficult and in some cases falls short of their potential.

Maria is an eighth grade student whose physical development had surpassed that of most of her peers. One day in school, her teacher asked her to share with the rest of the class an essay she thought was outstanding. When asked to stand and read it, Maria refused. The teacher was surprised and assumed the girl was shy or lacked self-confidence. Despite encouragement, the girl declined and sat quietly. In the room were three boys who had pointed and made remarks about her physical appearance. Maria would not put herself in a position to be further harassed.

Society is changing and no longer views sexual harassment as something to be tolerated or endured.

A person guilty of sexual harassment can also experience negative consequences. In addition to hurting the victim, a student who sexually harasses can be subject to school disciplinary procedures ranging from verbal reprimand to expulsion. Criminal proceedings may find the harasser guilty of a misdemeanor which carries with it possible fines, probation, or jail time. A disciplinary and criminal record can be serious obstacles to college entrance, career advancement, scholarship, or political positions, to name a few.

Society is changing and no longer views sexual harassment as something to be tolerated or endured. Such abusive behaviors have resulted in numerous social problems that affects all of society. When harassment is not confronted early in life, it can spread and become more intense, leading to abusive situations. For example, sexual harassment of young girls by young boys, in which girls are degraded, can eventually lead to more extreme abuse and even physical violence. In some cases, sex has become a battle ground between boys and girls, men and women.

Russell A. Sabella, Ph.D. & Robert D. Myrick, Ph.D.

Rocky Relationships and Domestic Violence

It is a sad fact that many boys grow to be men who take out their anger and frustrations with life on women. These inadequate men invariably grew up believing that women are weak and worthless beings who are to be dominated and used for their own purposes. There has probably never been a case of domestic violence against women where the men did not have a history of sexual harassment. When harassment and dysfunctional personalities are mixed, the result often ends in a violent and uncaring expression of disrespect and aggression.

Domestic violence of men against women is escalating. Look at these dismal statistics:

...mutual respect is the primary issue and it must begin early in life....

- Every fifteen seconds a woman is beaten by her husband or boyfriend.

- Thirty percent of women who are homicide victims are killed by husbands or boyfriends.

- Each year, more than four thousand women are killed in domestic violence situations.

- Women are in nine times more danger at home than they are on the streets.

Decent men share with women their outrage when they hear these statistics. Sympathetic and caring men speak of these issues with sensitivity and want to be a part of resolving a disconcerting social problem. They know that mutual respect is the primary issue and it must begin early in life, especially when young people are developing social skills and learning how to relate with others.

When harassers are confronted, they often claim they were "just kidding." They respond, "Can't you take a joke?" or "I didn't mean anything by it." The "just kidding" disclaimer is a common defense. It's possible some may have intended their actions to be funny or some form of playfulness. "Whatever gave you that idea?" remarked one girl who confronted a boy about some of his suggestive remarks she considered crude and childish, as well as insulting. She later remarked to her counselor, "Where do boys get off on the idea that girls like to be treated so rudely?"

Part of the answer to her question is found in the messages young people pick up from popular entertainment. Television, music, and movies provide numerous examples of lewd remarks, suggestive touches, and other forms of sexual harassment. In 1990 researchers at the University of Dayton in Dayton, Ohio found that sexual harassment was routine behavior on TV, especially the prime-time situation comedies or sitcoms. In most cases, the shows portray harassment as humorous and flippant, and they minimized or misrepresented its seriousness. Moreover, the actions were also reinforced by laugh tracks or by the lack of consequences for those who harassed. Confrontation was almost nonexistent.

While it was doubtful that the television writers deliberately wrote sexual harassment into the scripts, the study emphasized how they relied on stereotypical images of men and women to generate laughs. "It's just fun. We're just kidding around." In doing so, they sanctioned and encouraged sexual harassment. (Some musical groups that appeared on TV have delighted in singing songs that demean women, making them the target of ridicule.)

A national children's advocacy group called "Children Now," surveyed ten- to sixteen-year-olds about how television shapes their values. More than two-thirds of the young people said they were influenced by television. Seventy-seven percent said there is too much sex before marriage depicted, and 62 percent said sex on television and in movies influences their peers to have sexual relations when they are too young. The survey concluded that what most children see on television encourages them to take part in sexual activity too soon, to show disrespect for their parents, to lie, and to engage in aggressive behavior (*Los Angeles Times,* January 27, 1995).

Another contributing factor of harassment among children is that behavior is modeled for them by adults or adolescents. In addition to TV, movies, and popular music, they may see and hear abusive actions in their own homes or neighborhoods. They watch harassers exploit others. This creates an atmosphere that condones such behavior and portrays it as normal and appropriate. This is especially true when the inappropriate behavior is unchallenged.

An additional reason children harass their peers is because of their own insecurities about sexuality. It might be a case of showing off to other kids or attempts to suggest they know something about sex even though, in reality, it shows they know very little about it.

...what most children see on television encourages them to take part in sexual activity too soon....

Russell A. Sabella, Ph.D. & Robert D. Myrick, Ph.D.

Anita Hill Meets the Spur Posse

Anita Hill, a law professor at the University of Oklahoma, testified during the confirmation hearing for Supreme Court Justice Clarence Thomas in 1991 that he sexually harassed her in the 1980s. Her senate testimony put sexual harassment in the national spotlight. Although her credibility was attacked and Thomas was eventually approved for the Court, the public never forgot the confrontation. She later said that by ignoring harassment, we teach children it is okay. "We are reinforcing behavior, telling women you have to just put up with it, because the teacher, principal, or counselor won't do anything about it." She continued, "Gender attitudes must be molded in childhood. How do we educate men who just don't get it? Start when they are boys."

...not going to take it any more.

Following her testimony, many women began to speak up. The number of discrimination claims filed with the Office of Economic Opportunity increased six fold within a few months. The nation heard complaints from every state, as women increasingly voiced their concerns and said they were not going to take it any more.

About the same time in California, a group of high school boys received notoriety because of their competitive game of seeing who could "score" the most with girls. As members of a group called the Spur Posse, they earned points given by the group's leaders for their sexual conquests of girls. The boys called the girls "sluts" and said they weren't the most popular ones, as if this was some kind of justification for their actions. Some parents of the boys tried to defend them with a "boys will be boys" disclaimer and one or two parents complained the girls harassed the boys with their telephone calls.

What does it say when girls were willing to have sex with a member of the Spur Posse? Although some were forced, others were so desperate to be popular they willingly participated in sex. An American Association of University Women study entitled *The AAUW Report: How Schools Shortchange Girls* (1992), showed that girls' self-esteem drops as they enter adolescence, which can make them more vulnerable to tolerating and accepting sexual harassment and abuse.

The Dirt Patrol

A middle school girl named Sandra told her counselor how much she disliked walking down a certain school hallway. There was a group of boys who made her feel as if she was running a gauntlet. As she walked by, they would talk loudly among themselves about the curves in her sweater. One boy held up his hands about chest high, spreading and wiggling his fingers, and acting as if he were going to lunge toward her breasts. The more she tried to ignore them, the more they would step in her path and make suggestive remarks.

Sandra hated the boys but didn't know what to do. She was embarrassed by the attention they gave her and dreaded going to her class at the end of that hallway. Sometimes she would go to her locker and pretend she was getting assignments, when she really was waiting for the last bell to ring so she would not have to encounter the boys. She was often late to class. One day the teacher asked her why she was tardy so much, but Sandra simply shrugged her shoulders. The teacher replied, "Well, young lady, you had better figure it out because from now on points are going to be deducted from your grade if you are not here on time. Your coming in late day after day causes too many interruptions." About that time, another girl who was standing nearby spoke up and said, "It's the Dirt Patrol. They make her late to class. They're just a bunch of stupid boys who hang out together and think it's cool to pick on girls."

...education at an early age, before the problem occurs.

The teacher turned to Sandra and asked if she was being harassed on her way to class, but Sandra could say nothing. She looked down, uncertain and embarrassed, hoping she would not be asked to tell what the boys were saying or doing. "Well," the teacher said, "let's find out more about this little group who patrol the hallways," and she made a mental note to ask the school counselor and principal to investigate the matter.

The problem and impact of sexual harassment pervades the workplace, our colleges, universities, and our children. The negative consequences of sexual harassment can come in the form of emotional and personal turmoil, monetary damages, economic shrinkage, and barriers to career advancement. Such ramifications should not be accepted. Rather, further understanding and direct confrontation of the problem is in order. Efforts should include education at an early age, before the problem occurs.

Sexual Harassment: Confronting the Problem

The problem of sexual harassment could easily be ignored. It has been overlooked in many places for generations. However, times change and there is no better time than now to confront the issue. One problem related to change is the persistence of sex role stereotypes and common myths.

Sex Role Stereotypes

A Collision Course

Femininity and masculinity are attitudes and behavior patterns that have for centuries guided the lives of men and women. These sex roles shape many of the decisions which people make. As babies become toddlers and then preschoolers, they are deluged with direct and indirect messages about how they are to behave based solely on their gender. These messages come from parents and relatives, other adults, siblings, friends, and from cultural media such as television, books, and song lyrics.

...sex roles shape many of the decisions which people make.

In past decades, girls learned early on they should "not make waves," "be pretty and quiet," "please others," and "be sweet." From such expectations, many girls proceeded along a path of passivity and congeniality. They learned they were supposed to be tolerant and yield to others' needs, even if it meant sacrificing their own. Many developed a sense of physical and intellectual helplessness. They were discouraged from becoming self-reliant and independent. They relied on men to provide them with social status, protection, and a secure future.

Many of these same expectations still persist and may be the root of sexual harassment. For example, if a woman is too friendly, some men are likely to think that she is trying to seduce them. Or, if she is wearing a short skirt, then she wants the man to touch or comment on her legs.

Many boys are steered onto an "aggression" track that guides them toward a self-centered view of their place in the world. They learn to set aside the needs of others, to use physical responses to beat an opponent when faced with conflict, and to equate showing empathy with being weak and feminine. This training often leads to beliefs about sexual entitlement and social superiority over females. The result is a string of myths that boys and men are expected to live up to.

Moving toward open and nonconfining roles is not easy.

Given these dissimilar patterns, some of the travelers on the "niceness" track and some of those on the "aggression" track are on a collision course with each other. They may collide as preteens or teenagers in middle or high schools or at after-school jobs. They may experience a collision as young single adults in college or the work place. The "niceness" and "aggression" tracks may finally meet in the course of a marriage partnership, during dates, or even during a friendship in later years. Many of the collisions may be perceived, considered, or identified as sexual harassment. Thus, for many men and women, "the battle of the sexes" may be just that. From their socialization in childhood and adolescence, they developed different goals related to sexuality which set them up as adversaries.

Moving toward open and nonconfining roles is not easy. Teens who try to challenge these stereotypes usually don't get much support from their peers, society, and sometimes their own parents. Girls are told that boys won't like them if they show their intelligence. Boys are told that they are "wimps" if they don't fit the stereotype of the tough-guy "macho" male. A good start in being less constricted by gender roles is to become more aware of the options.

The Myths of Harassment

Some social myths attempt to justify and excuse sexual harassment. They can teach victims to blame themselves. They support the use of hostility as a mechanism for keeping females powerless and advocate that the prevention of sexual harassment is a woman's responsibility. Little sympathy is found in myths for victims who are so careless as to allow themselves to be sexually harassed.

Many myths perpetuate a "blame-the-victim" attitude and spare harassers of any guilt. They do not see harassment as serious or understand its consequences. Thus, the harasser is free to commit a similar crime in the future.

The Way We Never Were

Some people blame the surge of interest in sexual harassment on new legislation passed in recent years. They say, "This is not a big deal. It is something that has been going on for a long time and now, because of new laws, we have criminalized it." What they do not acknowledge is that the problems from sexual harassment are not new. People have experienced the damaging effects of sexual harassment for many years.

Others speak of the "good old days when people were treated with respect.... I remember when women were held on a pedestal and men protected their honor and rights." Yet, a close examination of history indicates that many women tolerated sexual harassment and viewed it as part of the way things were. Some were afraid to speak out while others accepted it as part of the way in which women were stereotyped.

What is new is the way we recognize, understand, and discuss the problem. Women are now feeling more empowered to discuss and confront sexual harassment. Men are more sensitive to the issue and willing to take a stern look at their own behavior. People in general are more open and receptive to discussing an age-old problem.

You Get What You Deserve

The "you get what you deserve" myth suggests that the victims incite harassment. This myth recognizes that the experience of the victim is traumatic yet it holds the victim responsible. Sexual harassment has sometimes been considered doubtful if a woman: dressed attractively; walked alone past a construction site; was, in the perpetrator's perception, a tease; had previous dates with a man; or simply smiled and said "hello." If harassment followed, it was considered the victim's fault. This myth about sexual harassment being enticed implies that the victim may have been playing a risky game of sexuality, and once in the game, is responsible for whatever happens.

Boys Will Be Boys

"Georgie Porgy Puddin' Pie, kissed the girls and made them cry." This popular children's rhyme has been passed down through the ages as something whimsical and funny. People now recognize that it involves teasing that is fun for one person at the expense of the other, especially the female. What should be expected of boys? Certainly, disrespectful behavior can no longer be accepted as a developmental stage. Boys need to learn how to develop positive relationships with girls in which both genders are valued and respected.

The Absence of "No" Doesn't Mean "Yes"

When sexual harassment is confronted, sometimes the perpetrator simply ignores it and continues.

Another myth is that the victim should have just said "no," or "stop." This myth involves poor or inaccurate communication. Victims of sexual harassment may sometimes say "yes" or do nothing simply because they are too frightened to confront the harasser who is often aggressive. In the case of a female victim, sometimes she may have difficulties in confronting sexual harassment because she has been socialized to be "nice" which usually means "do not make waves." Frequently, confronting sexual harassment is difficult because the victim may suffer unpleasant consequences such as negative peer pressure, ridicule, or isolation.

When sexual harassment is confronted, sometimes the perpetrator simply ignores it and continues. Perpetrators may believe that their behaviors were not so serious. They may not be able to understand why their actions were unwelcome. One Philadelphia woman kept saying "no" to a man after he lifted her shirt and bra, locked his college dorm room, pushed her on the bed, and removed her underwear. The woman did not try to escape or try to fight; he did not use any force. Under Pennsylvania law, the man in this situation did not commit sexual assault. The thought and sentiment of many rape victim advocates was, "What is it about the word 'no' that people don't understand?"

Something to be Endured

The problem of sexual harassment has sometimes been treated as one of life's growing pains similar to that of puberty. Members of society have made remarks such as, "It's just a part of life" or "It's something everyone goes through." Believing this is like believing "everyone gets robbed now and then so don't worry about it; just ignore it and get on with your life." A similar and common myth about sexual harassment is that rules, policies, or the laws prohibiting it restrict normal socializing between males and females. The truth is that sexual harassment consists of unwelcome conduct of a sexual nature. It in no way affects ordinary social contact between people (Petrocelli & Repa, 1992).

Beauty is the Beast

Another misconception about sexual harassment includes the "beauty" and "clothing" myths. Essentially, some people believe that a female's beauty can be so overpowering as to "cause" sexual harassment. Similarly, the victim can be blamed for the harassment because of the clothing she wore. In reality, although a woman's clothing may communicate, "I'm a woman," this is not the same message as "Touch me." Clothing does not give others permission to touch or grab; it does not signal what a woman wants or will do (Sandler, 1989).

The beauty and clothing myth views sexual harassment as an extension of biological drives, ignoring the more central issue of power, and shifting the responsibility and blame to the victim. Even in the case of prostitution—whereby a prostitute intends to dress in a way that is sexually attractive and elicits feelings of sexual desire—touching, grabbing, or other forms of sexual attention is not always wanted. If prostitutes are not satisfied with certain sexual bargains and do not give consent, they too can become victims of sexual harassment. There are no records of any person having suffered physiological, psychological, or any other damages because of not fulfilling sexual desires instilled by their "raging" hormones.

The beauty and clothing myth may also perpetuate the idea that the world is really a safe and fair place, and if the woman dresses or acts in a particular way, the male will control himself and not sexually harass her. In essence, this myth tells women that they must strive for invisibility to avoid being sexually harassed, and if they are sexually harassed, it is because they were not invisible enough. In reality, people are often sexually harassed regardless of their level of attractiveness, age, or behavior (Sandler, 1989).

Clothing does not give others permission to touch or grab; it does not signal what a woman wants or will do.

It's Not a Big Deal

Another myth which removes sexual harassment from being "real" denies that any harm was done. Unwanted behaviors such as "cat calling," lewd and lascivious comments, sexual innuendos, and jokes are dismissed as harmless flirting. This myth rejects the victim's trauma of experiencing another's intrusive actions. According to Burt (1991), many "no harm done" incidents refer to women who are devalued by society or women who are stereotyped as sexually available. The most extreme implication of this myth is that once a woman has consented to any sexual activity, she is never again in a position where she can legitimately say "no." Prostitutes are a special case of the open territory victim, so devalued that many people, once again, incorrectly believe that prostitutes cannot be sexually harassed.

The "it's not a big deal" myth is the type that can trap some people whose experiences of sexual violation are not taken seriously because they are stereotyped as being promiscuous and therefore already devalued. Any group of women stereotyped as being sexually active outside of marriage, such as divorcees or prostitutes, or any women who frequent places associated with being sexually available, such as bars, run the risk of being dismissed as unworthy of the law's protection or of sympathetic concern when they press charges of sexual harassment (Burt, 1991).

It Was Her Fault

The "she wanted it" myth maintains that the victim of sexual harassment wanted it, invited it, or liked it. The issue of consent lies at the center of this type of myth. It poses questions such as: Did she want it or did she have to survive it? Did her behavior result from personal motivation, in which case she grants permission, or from a hostile environment created by the perpetrator, in which case it is sexual harassment.

...myths contribute to the problem. They must be confronted....

Many myths concerning women and sex are distilled to a belief that "she never means no." At some level, women are always presumed to "want it," no matter what is said. To differentiate sexual harassment from flirting, one must be convinced that the victim did not consent to the sexual actions of another or others. Differentiation becomes further convoluted when women with certain stereotypical reputations or identities are assumed to consent more readily, to more men, in more situations.

These and other myths contribute to the problem of sexual harassment. They must be confronted as part of developing new ways in which people relate to one another.

Sexual Harassment: Helping Resolve the Problem

People do not walk around harassing one another all day long. Harassment is a time or an event in which the perpetrator acts in an inappropriate way. Sometimes it becomes a habit and the person is not even aware of what is happening or the message that is being sent. What happens in those situations? What causes or influences a person to harass someone?

What makes some people do the things they do? Why do some children grow up to be responsible citizens while others tend to choose activities that put them in conflict with others and which make them less productive? It is generally accepted that while most people are given a certain genetic structure which can influence life experiences, personality development is the critical factor that determines social acceptance and success.

Social and economic factors, racial and ethnic background, and even birth order are considered determinants of personality. Other major sources identified are: 1) impressions that a young person receives from significant others (e.g., parents, teachers, siblings, and peers; 2) life-values that are presented and then incorporated into one's self-concept; 3) ability to judge one's self and others by both his or her own standards, as well as common-sense beliefs advocated by a society; and, 4) opportunities to learn from life experiences and integrate them into perceptions of reality.

Teachers and facilitators need to be aware of children's developmental stages and their personal backgrounds. Motivations, expectations, needs and interests, are a part of developing a positive personality. On occasion, personalities take a negative turn and, perhaps because of a lack of education or other disadvantages, an individual tends to behave in socially inappropriate ways. When such behavior is repeated frequently, then a pattern emerges and goes beyond being a habit. It may be integrated into a personality type or profile.

Four Personality Profiles

...some people have a greater proclivity, or tendency, to engage in sexual harassment.

Research suggests that there are no conclusive personality factors that determine whether or not a person will become a harasser. However, studies do indicate that some people have a greater proclivity, or tendency, to engage in sexual harassment. It might be helpful to examine four personality profiles, although they are not necessarily mutually exclusive, that are typically associated with the issue. This might provide additional insight in both understanding and resolving the problem.

The Personally Inadequate Harasser

Persons who commit sexual harassment because of feeling inadequate usually do not know of a better way to say, "I am somebody special and important." They have a low level of self-esteem and attempt to compensate. Rather than trying to uplift themselves to the level of others with higher self-esteem, they try to drag others down to their own level. They hurt others to make themselves feel better about who they are.

The Power Hungry Harasser

This harasser experiences a power imbalance with others, and similar to the inadequate harasser, attempts to compensate. This individual tries to tip the scales of control and be on top. Often times a male, the harasser may try to fulfill a sex-role stereotype of male dominance and control. In a society that is working to empower both genders, this person fails to understand the value of equality and shared privileges. This harasser believes that others are of less value and do not deserve to have an equal part in decision making.

The Angry and Aggressive Harasser

Some harassers are bullies. They like to hurt others and intimidate them. They enjoy humiliating victims because it gives them a sense of personal satisfaction, which is often related to low self-esteem and lack of affect.

The pleasure they experience in their angry and aggressive actions may be associated with hurtful experiences in their own lives, perhaps times when they were bullied, physically or verbally abused, and treated with disrespect. In some cases, the aggressive child lacks common social skills. In many cases the harassers are insensitive to the feelings and needs of others.

Russell A. Sabella, Ph.D. & Robert D. Myrick, Ph.D.

The Copy Cat Harasser

Social behavior is learned. Small children watch and listen to parents and significant others in order to learn how to act. Actions which are rewarded are often carried out more frequently, intensely, and for longer periods. Actions followed by discomfort or pain usually cease after some time.

A behavior may be learned and imitated because the behavior being viewed was rewarded. Through vicarious learning, an individual might watch an act of sexual harassment which was followed by supportive laughter and encouragement from others. This increases the chance that such viewed behavior will be imitated.

...harassment is derived from personal deficiencies.

It can be helpful to know how certain personalities have a tendency to disrespect the rights of the others and that harassment is derived from personal deficiencies. Some individuals will need special counseling or therapy to work through their problems and to gain a new perspective on life. They will need more intensive work in order to reshape their personalities. However, personality changes and development can begin with educational activities that help a person learn new ways of interacting with others.

One teacher, who was irritated by a young man's personal style, concluded that he was probably going to be in trouble for the rest of his life and that sexual harassment would fit his style. It was a discouraging prediction. "I've tried everything with him and nothing works. He simply has a rotten attitude about others. Admittedly, his family doesn't help much and he is in a bad situation, but that is no excuse for some of his inappropriate behavior and that should not be tolerated." The teacher is right in many respects. The boy's home environment may be a problem and, with a lack of positive models, he may be developing a hostile attitude about others, but this does not mean that he should be excused for his insensitivity and disrespect of others. It does mean that the boy needs more education and opportunities to practice effective social skills.

Related Issues

Certainly personality development and social expectations deserve attention when confronting sexual harassment. There are some other related issues that also need to be considered when helping resolve the problem.

"Crying Wolf": False Accusations

Some people believe that many charges of sexual harassment are false and that real cases are rare. Although it is true that a person can be falsely accused of sexual harassment, this is a small percentage of all incidents. To the contrary, studies indicate that sexual harassment is widespread. Reports on the prevalence and incidence of sexual harassment are thought to still be highly underestimated (Harris, 1993). Sandler (1989) reported that females—perhaps more than ninety percent—don't want to report or file charges because they know of the risks involved. Risks may include retaliation from the perpetrator, being ostracized from peers or colleagues, ridiculed, additionally harassed by others, and sometime the loss of employment or promotion.

Lack of Reports

According to Harris (1994), students do not routinely report sexual harassment incidents to adults. In addition, boys who have been harassed are more likely than girls to have told no one (27% and 19%, respectively). Only seven percent of sexually harassed students say they have told a teacher about the experience, with girls twice as likely as boys to have done this. By far, most reporting takes place on a peer-to-peer basis: 63% of sexually harassed students have told a friend.

Reasons for the lack of reporting include the belief that victims feel uncomfortable, embarrassed, or ashamed.

Reasons for the lack of reporting include the belief that victims feel uncomfortable, embarrassed, or ashamed. They are afraid that no one will believe them, that harassment will reflect badly on their character, that somehow they will be viewed as having invited the behavior. And often, they do blame themselves. They may feel unjustified guilt, be fearful of repercussions, and may even be too ashamed to tell friends or family (Sandler, 1989). If students received greater permission, support, and were more knowledgeable and confident about reporting, perhaps it might occur more often.

Reporting sexual harassment is important for several reasons. One, even if the victim does not press criminal charges, the incident is officially documented. Second, reporting sexual harassment to school and law enforcement officials can help the victim feel more empowered.

Third, reporting is the first step in an official investigation and a possible conviction. Inconsistent and nonexistent consequences for perpetrators of sexual harassment supports further, and sometimes more frequent, sexually harassing behaviors to occur.

Fourth, reporting an incident of sexual harassment can lead to a confrontation with the perpetrator and ultimately to a resolution. A successful resolution can help to avoid further actions and it can prove to be an educational experience. Such an experience can become constructive and reduce the risk of another incident. Last, reporting sexual harassment may reduce the risk of the perpetrator victimizing the same person or other individuals.

The Need for a Policy Statement

As the courts continue to address the problem of sexual harassment, schools have responded with policies and procedures that are more inclusive and action oriented. An effective sexual harassment policy helps people better understand what sexual harassment is and what it is not. It assists students, parents, faculty, and other school staff to acknowledge that sexual harassment is against school rules and law. Policies are effective when they are fair, describe appropriate consequences, and offer resources. They outline proper procedures for resolution and include an acceptable time frame for arriving at a resolution.

Policies are effective when they are fair, describe appropriate consequences, and offer resources.

A well written policy can help schools better establish and maintain an atmosphere of zero-tolerance for such sexual harassment. Students and parents can be more confident that the school is a safe and secure place to work and learn. An effective policy does not allow sexual harassment to be perpetuated through passivity and disregard. It establishes a clear stance against it while attempting to prevent victimization and possible litigation.

Susan Strauss (1992) outlined guidelines for developing a sexual harassment policy and procedure. Among them were:

A. A philosophy statement, definition, list of specific behaviors that constitute sexual harassment, and sanction for the harasser;

B. A statement of confidentiality, options for informal resolution, and a specific time frame for resolution;

C. A statement dealing with retaliation, a grievance procedure, and a statement regarding appeals and alternative complaint procedures;

D. A statement regarding training for staff and students, a plan to involve students, and a plan to communicate the policy, procedure, and programs to the community.

A possible outline for an effective policy may include items that address the following:

- **How is sexual harassment defined?** A clear, concise and comprehensive definition is needed, with a few specific examples.

- **What impact does it have on others?** Personal consequences such as feelings of confusion, embarrassment, guilt, lack of self-confidence, isolation, powerless, scared, hopeless, and anger may be cited. Examples of physical ailments might be included. This section might also cite court settlements and ways in which harassment detracts from the learning and work environment.

- **What can be done about it?** Possible options can be outlined, such as confronting the perpetrator, talking with friends, keeping a written record of events, seeking help from others, and requesting help from school officials and resource personnel.

- **How can a person be helped?** Include topics such as being a good listener, discussing choices, encouraging a person to seek assistance from others, and being available as support.

- **What are some questions that can be asked?** A self-evaluation of behavior may be appropriate.

- **What are the common obstacles to seeking help?** List some items that often prevent people from taking action or reporting harassment, including their fears and apprehensions and the uncertainty of next steps.

- **What are some referral sources?** A list of available resources and referral sources is valuable, especially sensitive adults who have been trained to respond to cases of sexual harassment.

Caring People Can Help

Caring about the success of our children and their future must be expressed by our words and actions.

Teachers, counselors, administrators, parents, and peers can help confront sexual harassment. Caring about the success of our children and their future must be expressed by our words and actions.

Teachers Can Help

Teachers are in a good position to conduct intervention efforts for reducing the risk of sexual harassment. They can facilitate activities, lessons, and discussions which enhance knowledge, caring attitudes, and behaviors that foster healthy relationships. They can do this in their own classes or as part of a teacher-as-advisor program (TAP). Some advantages are:

- Classroom groups are already intact, usually uniform for grade level.
- Trust and genuineness is part of the teacher-student relationship which is an important ingredient with a sensitive topic such as sexual harassment.
- Students have had the opportunity to establish rapport with the teacher and with each other. Increased rapport is essential to discussing sexual harassment and engaging in experiential activities.
- The unit can provide further development of the helping relationship with students and sometimes even parents.
- Teachers can model effective communication and acceptable behaviors.
- Since the learning activities focus on developing and maintaining healthy relationships, it can be a positive experience for the teacher.

Counselors Can Help

School counselors work with students individually and in groups. They can give special attention to both harassers and victims, seeking causes and resolutions. They can also:

- Lead small group counseling units about boy/girl relationships.
- Talk privately with students involved in sexual harassment cases.
- Consult and support teachers who are integrating curricula that addresses the problem and issues of sexual harassment.
- Serve as a school wide complaint coordinator.
- Help train and coordinate peer facilitator programs, with special attention to peer helper projects that focus on student relationships.
- Present and encourage the use of developmental guidance units about sexual harassment.
- Conduct in-service sessions for teachers.

Peers Can Help

Peer facilitators may be an ideal resource for helping. Consider that adults sometimes make children feel uncomfortable, especially when talking about a sensitive topic such as sexual conduct. Frequently, people feel others their own age can better understand what they are going through, and a better understanding usually results in more effective help.

Everyone knows the weight a peer carries behind any message, positive or negative, can be greater than that of an adult. Young people listen best to other young people. The positive influence peer facilitators can have on middle school students is powerful and exciting. There are other advantages of being a peer facilitator involved in sexual harassment risk reduction. Peers are often more accessible and available. As activists, peers can alert adults to student needs and concerns in the area of sexual harassment. Using professionally and systematically trained peer facilitators increases the number of helpers and the magnitude of the message.

Frequently, people feel others their own age can better understand what they are going through....

After some fundamental training, peer facilitators can participate in various kinds of helping projects. There are four different helping roles around which peer facilitators can perform: student assistant, tutor, special friend, and small group leader (Myrick & Folk, 1991).

Student Assistants work with teachers and counselors around classrooms and in the guidance or main office. The assistants can greet visitors to the school, answer telephones, take messages to teachers and students, construct bulletin boards informing the public about sexual harassment, help collect or distribute materials or information in workshops and around the school, and work on routine office or classroom tasks. Although there is some interaction between the peer facilitators and teachers or students, this role is generally confined to providing assistance to peers.

Peer Tutors work with other students to improve their work in academic subjects. Peer facilitators working as peer tutors provide a new kind of helping relationship, one that begins by acknowledging what the person is experiencing and how feelings and ideas about self and school enter into studying. This role is especially helpful for a student who has experienced sexual harassment and can use some extra academic support.

Special Friends are peer facilitators who try to develop a close helping relationship with another student. This friendship can make the difference for some students who feel uninvolved, left-out, or alienated from school, especially as a result of experiencing sexual harassment. Peer facilitators who take on the role of special friend learn how to be good listeners and how to treat matters privately. There will be times when they will confront individuals, perhaps encouraging them to seek help from an adult or professional. There may even be times when the peer helper refers someone to a school counselor, or to someone who has authority, or to someone with resources to help.

Russell A. Sabella, Ph.D. & Robert D. Myrick, Ph.D.

Small Group Leaders are peer facilitators make learning experiences for others more personal and exciting. It can be boring and frustrating to be in a large group and have few opportunities to be heard. Most students want to talk with others about their ideas and share their opinions. Classes with 30 or more students in attendance leave little time for everyone to talk and to be heard unless large groups are organized into smaller ones.

When that leader is a trained peer facilitator, the group members are more likely to stay on task....

In order to have small groups work efficiently, there must be a designated group leader. When that leader is a trained peer facilitator, the group members are more likely to stay on task, to take turns sharing, and to accomplish group goals. For example, a classroom of 30 students can be divided into five groups of six students each. Five peer facilitators, each assigned to one of the groups, can follow the lead of the teacher or large group leader. At a certain time, the smaller groups can be assembled and each person might be encouraged to say at least one thing about the topic (e.g., a scenario about sexual harassment). Thus, all 30 students participate in a few minutes, rather than few who dominate a classroom discussion as others sit and listen.

Leading groups as a peer facilitator is also good leadership training. Many of the principles applied in this role can be used in other group situations, either as a designated group leader or as a group member who is trying to help facilitate the group.

The guidance unit presented in Chapter 5 was piloted with the assistance of high school peer facilitators who worked as co-group leaders. They met with a trainer, experienced the sessions, then reviewed interpersonal skills and a manual which outlined the activities. The structured activities made it easy for the leaders to present the unit and lead group discussions. Later, they talked about their experiences with their supervisor.

Starting a club or organization. You may want to start and sponsor a club or organization at your school that's mission is to facilitate the understanding and prevention of sexual harassment. Possible names for the group might be:

Teens Against Sexual Harassment (TASH)

Students Taking All Relationships Seriously (STARS)

Caring About Relationships Everywhere (CARE)

Honor, Esteem, and Respect Together (HEART)

Healthy Relationships Together (HEART)

Acting Responsibly Together (ART)

Heart To Heart (H2H)

Club members may be trained in facilitating the unit and additionally conduct projects which include:

- **Educational Talks:** Students are invited into other classrooms to present information about sexual harassment. They may conduct one or more of the activities included in the book.

- **Play or Creative Dramatics:** Students can create a short play or drama which demonstrates the problem of sexual harassment and includes possible solutions. These may be short case scenarios which are acted out. They may even be interactive and include different resolutions which the audience discusses.

- **Two-minute Talks on the School News:** Students are invited to give a two-minute talk about behaviors, attitude, and knowledge related to sexual harassment. They may do this once per week for the entire school year.

- **Educational Materials:** Students design 8 x 11 flyers that inform students about different aspects of sexual harassment prevention. The flyers are distributed throughout classrooms.

- **Bulletin Boards:** Students create designated bulletin boards about sexual harassment once every two to three weeks.

- **Anonymous Hotline:** Students create and operate a hotline by checking the hotline messages, filling out reports, and assisting the administration.

- **Raise Money for Charity:** Fund raisers can be conducted with proceeds going to a community service group that deals with violence reduction, especially sexual harassment.

- **Puppet Show:** Students create and perform a puppet show for younger students.

- **Publications:** Write and disseminate a brochure or pamphlet for the school or district that informs the public about sexual harassment including ways to prevent and resolve the problem.

Parents Can Help

A parent's involvement in a student's education is a strong factor in that child's success at school. This involvement is known to range from direct help with homework to involvement in other school based activities such as working with the Parent-Teacher Association. A parent can help to ensure that their child's school environment is free from sexual harassment by doing things such as:

- Teach your children attitudes and behaviors, beginning at an early age, that lead to healthy, mutually respectful, and flexible relationships.

- Listen carefully to your child when talking about sexual harassment. It is easy to blame the victim. "I told you not to wear those kinds of clothes to school. What did you expect?!"

- Ask school personnel about their sexual harassment policy, procedures, and protocol. Make certain that it is comprehensive and deals with the problem in a timely manner.

- Be supportive of a zero-tolerance policy for sexual harassment.

- Speak with administrators about concerns regarding sexual harassment. Often times a parent's words will fall harder on the ears of decision makers than if they came from a teacher or counselor.

- Take time to understand the problem of sexual harassment. Talk to others, read the literature about it, and ask questions. Sexual harassment can be confusing.

The problem of sexual harassment will not disappear on its own.

Sexual harassment is highly recognized as a pervasive and robust problem. On the job, in our schools, and across places where people meet, it is proving to be quite costly. Sexual harassment scorns its victims, hinders people's careers and opportunities for advancement, and has a depleting effect on our job performance and productivity. The problem of sexual harassment will not disappear on its own. Nor will it go away if we simply ignore it. It is a problem that must be dealt with head on with education, hard work, and persistence.

School Administrators Can Help

Superintendents, principals, assistant principals, and other administrators can be pivotal people in the movement to reduce the risk of sexual harassment among our youth.

- Recognize that sexual harassment happens in our schools. It is no longer known to be a problem in only universities and the workplace.

- Be comfortable in talking about it with others, especially the children. Remember that most children are already familiar with the general ideas about sexual harassment and only are in need of the details.

- Encourage in-service training among school personnel to help recognize and understand the problem of sexual harassment.

- Help to develop strong policies, procedures, and protocol in the schools.

- Support the efforts of teachers and counselors in conducting guidance and counseling activities designed to address the problem of sexual harassment.

- Work with school attorneys to ensure that all gender equity laws are properly satisfied.

- Make certain that sexual harassment complaints are dealt with in a timely and appropriate manner.

- Help foster a zero-tolerance atmosphere among students, faculty, staff, and parents.

Helping students receive the best education possible, which includes attention to social and personal development, is the goal of all school administrators. They must manage limited resources, address faculty needs, and listen to parent interests and concerns. It is not always easy to introduce a new program, even though it benefits students and others, and even though it fosters a more productive learning atmosphere. Some frequently asked questions, and possible responses, include:

1. **I'm worried that as the students go though the unit, I'll have dozens of them screaming "sexual harassment." I don't have the staff to handle such a situation. What would I do?**

   - The unit presented in this book, and those similar to it, have been used in different schools and classrooms. There were no reported cases of administrators complaining that the learning experience resulted in any significant problems. To the contrary, one teacher reported that the unit

Russell A. Sabella, Ph.D. & Robert D. Myrick, Ph.D.

provided one victim with the "tools" to deal with the problem. Additionally, the guidance unit about sexual harassment focuses on what sexual harassment is and what it is not. The unit emphasizes that falsely accusing someone of sexual harassment constitutes criminal behavior and can be met with significant disciplinary consequences.

2. **What if a parent objects to such a sensitive topic being taught in school?**

   • Parental objection to the unit should be met with sensitivity and diplomacy. Right or wrong, for better or for worse, a parent has a right to decide what kinds of guidance and counseling activities that their child experiences. Although the unit can be conducted as part of a comprehensive guidance and counseling curriculum, health, or other curriculum, parent permission to participate may alleviate any negative responses. Some principals have given the unit to active parent volunteers or the PTA to review and make suggestions that were later tailored for their individual school.

3. **What if, as a result of the unit, one of my teachers is accused of sexual harassment?**

   • The majority of sexual harassment occurs between and among peers. However, in some cases, an adult (e.g., teacher, secretary, custodial worker, cafeteria personnel) may be accused of sexually harassing a student. If this happens, it should be treated seriously and dealt with in a timely manner. It is not an easy situation to deal with, especially if the adult is popular and known to otherwise be effective in his or her job. It is not a pleasant task for a supervisor to confront an employee about possible sexual harassment and to inquire; yet, it is necessary. If ignored, there is a chance that the problem could continue, and the school may be subject to a law suit.

4. **Is the unit best conducted with groups homogenous for gender?**

   • The advantage of presenting the unit to any one gender is that conversation might be less inhibited or embarrassing. The disadvantage is that the discussion is more limited and restricted in regard to differing viewpoints. The other advantage of mixed gender is that such groups offer practice in intergender communication about sensitive topics.

5. **What if some faculty members are resistant to conducting the unit school-wide?**

   • Members of a faculty may become resistant to the idea of facilitating the unit on confronting sexual harassment if they: a) see it as extra work; b) fear that they do not have adequate knowledge about the topic; c) believe that they could not facilitate a discussion following the activities; or d) do not view sexual harassment as a problem in the school or society. These issues need to be addressed among adults who might lead the unit. Information and supporting statistics may help reduce resistance and provide a base for the intervention. Some cases might be cited, especially those that involved awarding victim(s) monetary damages. Emphasize that the unit includes materials and scripts which contribute to its success and that most participants have recommended it for other students.

6. **What should be done if a student is identified as a frequent harasser or scores low on the Sexual Harassment Inventory?**

   • Such a student could be referred to other specialists, perhaps a school counselor, to follow-up and explore the tendency of the student to victimize others. The unit and activities are designed to help prevent harassment from occurring and lay the foundation for helping students who enjoy victimizing others. The group experience increases awareness, knowledge, and helps change attitudes. It has been known to be sufficient "treatment" for a young person who is learning social skills.

7. **When can the unit be conducted?**

   • The unit is designed as a preventative measure and should be conducted as early in the school year as possible. However, it is never too late to help children reduce their risk of being involved in an incident or series of incidents involving sexual harassment. The unit can be presented as part of a teacher-advisor program or as a unit in a regularly scheduled academic course.

Russell A. Sabella, Ph.D. & Robert D. Myrick, Ph.D.

8. **What is the best way to handle a student who becomes disruptive during a session by inappropriately joking and making light of sexual harassment?**

   - Sometimes a student will joke and act out, disrupting the group process. Such students may be embarrassed by the topic, or may be nervous when discussing sexual harassment. Their discomfort might be expressed in inappropriate behavior. It may be necessary to confront immature and disruptive students in private, or it might be appropriate to simply draw attention to how difficult it can be for some students to talk about the matter. Personal counseling may be required.

9. **What if a student discloses in front of the group that he or she has been sexually harassed?**

   - This student is taking a risk and wants to be heard to be heard and supported. There is also a strong message being sent and the student has decided to take a stand. Congratulations might be in order for his or her courage and appreciation for enabling the group to consider a personal issue. The group might give the student feedback in terms of how they are reacting to the disclosure and a professional judgment is made regarding the exploration of details or an appropriate referral.

Russell A. Sabella, Ph.D. & Robert D. Myrick, Ph.D.

Confronting Sexual Harassment: A Guidance Unit

This section presents a guidance unit on sexual harassment that might be used with teenagers. It consists of eight sessions, each with suggested activities and guidelines for teachers or group facilitators. Reproducibles needed for each activity are included. Additional activities for supplemental experiences are presented in the next chapter.

Sexual harassment has been a problem typically recognized and studied in the workplace and across universities. Only recently has it been identified as a problem among our youth in their school environments. The following statistics reflect the extent of the problem:

- Four in five students (about 81%) say they have experienced some form of sexual harassment during their school lives; 85% of girls and 76% of boys.

- One in 3 students (32%) who have been harassed first experienced sexual harassment in grade six or earlier.

- Two in 3 of all students surveyed (66%) have been targets of sexual comments, jokes, looks, and gestures, as well as touching, grabbing, and/or pinching in a sexual way.

- Nearly 4 in 5 students (79%) who have been harassed have been targeted by peers—current or former students. Eighteen percent (18%) of students who have been harassed cite adults as the perpetrators.

- Two in 3 students who have been harassed (66%) said they had been harassed in the hallway.

Working with Teenagers

This is a critical time for shaping....

Working with teenagers early makes good sense. Ideally, intervention efforts are designed to preclude sexual harassment from happening. Research shows that initial experiences of sexual harassment occur from kindergarten through college. A small number, about seven percent, of students first experience it before the third grade. First time experiences of sexual harassment increase with grade level and peaks at about the seventh grade. After the seventh grade, initial experiences gradually decline. It is estimated that only one percent of eleventh grade students experience sexual harassment for the first time.

Younger students may be in the initial stages of developing attitudes, behaviors, and knowledge which can later influence whether they are involved in sexual harassment or not. This is a critical time for shaping such factors in a positive way which can ultimately contribute to healthy and happy relationships. Much unnecessary discomfort can be averted with systematic training.

Teenagers are also receptive to sexual harassment sensitivity and communication skills training. They find such discussions stimulating, refreshing, and for many victims, empowering. Their experiences are confirmed and explained. Also, many teenagers enjoy the fact that they have been trusted and considered mature enough to handle a sensitive subject. At this age, when interest in the other gender begins to flourish, boys and girls appreciate the help with the do's and don'ts of healthy relationships.

Working with teenagers in the area of sexual harassment risk reduction can also benefit the facilitator. Especially at the middle school level, quite often (approximately two-thirds of the time), students do not believe there is anyone in their school to whom they can talk about their problems. You will have the chance to show yourself as a caring and trustworthy individual. You can make great strides in the teacher-student relationship while helping students to feel further cared for, valued, and safe.

These learning activities include material designed to:

- Increase knowledge pertaining to sexual harassment, including legal and personal consequences.
- Heighten awareness of sexual harassment supportive beliefs.
- Better determine what sexual harassment is and what it is not.
- Enhance skills such as giving critical feedback, active listening, and officially reporting sexual harassment.
- Practice behaviors conducive to healthy, equitable relationships.

Working with Parents

Parents play an important part in the education of their children and want them to gain the most out of school. This includes both learning academic and social skills. Most parents see schools as the workplace of youth. They know that a positive working environment can make the difference in how much their children enjoy going to school and their productivity.

Sexual harassment can be confronted through a prevention approach, as suggested by the unit and activities in this book. It encourages students and parents to look at a problem that has been in existence for a long time but appears to be escalating in today's society. A typical response is to wait until the problem rears its ugly head and results in a crisis at school. An incident, for example, may happen where students are harassed, which then leads to an embarrassing confrontation that usually results in punitive consequences. Too often potential problems that linger in our schools are not addressed until a critical incident takes place and then a quick reaction is required.

In a proactive approach, students are given an opportunity to learn more about a social problem in advance of a crisis and, subsequently, steps can be taken to help reduce problem moments. If difficulties arise, for whatever reason, students who have discussed the related issues in advance are better able to help resolve the predicament.

A guidance unit is easily incorporated into the regular academic schedule, perhaps in an English or social studies class. The unit in this book might also be presented in a teacher-advisor program, where students and teachers have an opportunity to talk about the developmental concerns and needs of students. It could be used with a target population as either a counselor intervention or as a developmental guidance program.

Some parents will want to know how the unit and activities suggested in this book are related to helping their child learn.

Some parents will want to know how the unit and activities suggested in this book are related to helping their child learn. Discuss with them the costs of sexual harassment to the world of work and how it can also destroy a learning environment at school. Describe for them how some students will not participate in class, attend school, or interact with other students for fear of being harassed. Ask them to think of situations that have been portrayed recently on television or reported in the newspapers and magazines. Some may even recall times when they were harassed or witnessed it. Consult with them about their concerns.

Parents are encouraged to look at the unit in advance, if they choose, and to ask questions.

Parents are encouraged to look at the unit in advance, if they choose, and to ask questions. On occasion it might be necessary to tell parents about the unit at a school advisory meeting or through a school announcement. Those parents who do not want their children to participate in the unit have the right to withdraw them.

Most teachers, administrators, and parents quickly see how the unit is related to helping students gain the most from school and that it is related to academic performance. It gives students a chance to learn and practice problem-solving skills and parent permission is not required. However, on occasion it may be appropriate to obtain parent permission.

A sample parent permission form can be seen in Figure 5.1. We know that many teenagers forget to take permission slips home. Often times the forgetful ones are those who might benefit most from the unit. Parent permission slips can complicate the implementation of the program, because it is an extra step that involves time and more preparation. The unit is still a worthwhile project and after a few pilot experiences, there may be less need to get permission and more need to simply consult with concerned parents.

Figure 5.1

Sample Parent Permission Form

Dear Parent,

As you may know, sexual harassment is any unwanted sexual attention that interferes with a person's life. It has been known to be a problem in many communities, schools, and places of work. It disrupts effective learning and productivity.

Sexual harassment can have a negative impact on children's grades, attendance, and behavior as well as their dignity and esteem.

(Your School/District) has a zero-tolerance policy against sexual harassment in an effort to provide safe and secure learning environments for students. The problem can be prevented through education.

Please allow your child to participate in a developmental guidance unit entitled *Confronting Sexual Harassment*. The unit will be conducted once per week for ____ weeks and is designed to foster sensitive and respectful relationships among students.

If you have any questions or comments, please call _____.

Sincerely,

(Name of Counselor)

- -

Confronting Sexual Harassment
Parent Permission

I give permission for my son/daughter,
_____ , to participate in a guidance unit about sexual harassment. I understand that not granting permission will in *no* way directly affect his or her grades or other school performance in any way.

_____

Parent Signature   Date

_____

Parent Signature   Date

Helpful Hints for Group Facilitators

As a group facilitator, it might be helpful to be reminded of these group procedure "tips" to enhance the success of the unit:

- Read the entire unit before beginning the first session. This will give you an overall "picture" of the objectives and how the sessions build on one another. Also, you may want to review and refresh your memory by skimming each session before leading it.

- Leave about six or seven minutes to conduct your closing questions and statements.

- Use high facilitative responses in all your interactions. Especially concentrate on making feeling-focused responses, clarifying and summarizing, and asking open-ended (how or what) questions for discussion.

- Move through the procedures of each session at a fast pace without sacrificing effectiveness; this keeps students' attention.

- Check the physical arrangement of the room before starting and make certain that it is favorable for making the plan work.

- Stick to the plan while maintaining a little flexibility to accommodate your own personal style.

Summary of Sessions

Session	Title	Session Focus
1	The Nature of the Beast	Knowledge
2	Go to Your Corner!	Knowledge & Attitude
3	Is it Sexual Harassment?	Knowledge & Attitude
4	The Web	Knowledge & Attitude
5	What are You Trying to Say?	Related Behaviors & Knowledge
6	Hey! You're in My Space!	Related Behaviors & Knowledge
7	Helping Yourself and Others	Related Behaviors & Knowledge
8	Moving Around and Moving On	Evaluation

Russell A. Sabella, Ph.D. & Robert D. Myrick, Ph.D.

Session 1: **The Nature of the Beast**

Objectives: To introduce and discuss the topic of boy-girl relationships and how physical changes influence personal relationships; to introduce the concept of sexual harassment and the extent of it being a problem in society.

Materials: "X's" and "O's" sheets (see Session 1 Reproducibles, pp. 154-155), masking tape.

Procedure:

Begin by saying...   *Good afternoon. (For Peer Facilitators: My name is _____.) Today is the first of six sessions that we are going to have together. We will be learning about a very important issue which faces us in our society. That issue is sexual harassment. Once a week for the next six weeks, we will be taking a look at what sexual harassment is, why it happens, and how to reduce the chances that it will happen. We will also learn what to do about sexual harassment if it happens to you or a friend.*

Then say...   *Let's think about a few questions to get started....*
- *What can you remember about the kinds of games that you played in elementary school?*
- *Did these involve primarily boys, girls, or both?*
- *How do physical changes in boys and girls at the middle and high school affect the way in which they talk and act toward each other?*

Now say...   *Nature plays a part in preparing boys and girls for more mature and closer relationships through physical changes. They cause confusion, embarrassment, uncertainty, shyness, aggression, and almost always some social awkwardness. The teenage years are a special time for boys and girls, when you have an opportunity to learn how to relate to others in positive ways.*

Next say...   *Some of the problems during this time evolve in the form of sexual harassment. This is a problem that some of you are already familiar with. Let's play a game of "Tic-Tac-Know" to learn more about the nature of sexual harassment.*

Activity 1.1: "Tic-Tac-Know!"

- Clear a part of the classroom to make room for the Tic-Tac-Know grid.
- Mark off your grid with the masking tape like so:

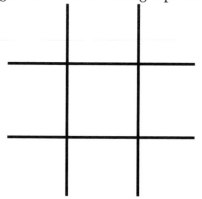

- Ask for volunteers to make up two different groups.
- Have the two groups stand on two opposite sides of the grid and ...

Then say...   *One team will be the X's and the other team will be the O's. You will hear a series of questions—some multiple choice, others true/false. Discuss these among your team and come to an agreement on the answer. If you are correct you get to choose a member of your team to walk into a spot on the grid and hold that position. If you are wrong you cannot put anyone on the grid and control goes back to the other team. The other team will get a new question. The first team to get Tic-Tac-Know wins! We'll move pretty quickly so we can play two games involving everyone in the class.*

- Read the following questions for each game. Each question has the correct answer and an explanation.
- After you tell each team whether their response to the question is correct or not, wait until they have picked a spot on the grid and have settled down to read the rationale. Only the person holding the X or the O can decide which spot on the grid to choose.

Questions for Tic-Tac-Know

1. Someone is being sexually harassed when another person makes a sexual comment about them.

   ANSWER: FALSE. The comment must be unwanted for it to be sexual harassment.

2. Nine times out of ten, when you ignore sexual harassment it usually goes away.

   ANSWER: FALSE. Ignoring it makes it happen more because the harasser does not recognize that the behavior is unwanted.

3. Even if a person meant something as a joke, it still can be considered sexual harassment if it is unwelcome.

   ANSWER: TRUE. Joking does not excuse unwanted sexual attention and certainly does not dismiss the act as sexual harassment.

4. Sexual harassment happens because some people are too sensitive and they don't like flirting.

   ANSWER: FALSE. Sexual harassment happens because the offender is ignorant, immature, or just plain mean. The victim is not to blame.

5. There are five different forms of sexual harassment.

   ANSWER: FALSE. There are three forms of sexual harassment which includes: Physical/visual (such as touching, brushing against, flicking one's tongue at someone). Quid pro quo means "this for that" and happens when someone wants to trade something for sex. Hostile environment is a form of sexual harassment when someone is subject to sexual comments or sexual materials (such as posters of naked people) that negatively affects his or her school performance.

6. Sexual harassment happens most often in (a) the hallways, (b) the classroom, or (c) in the parking lot.

   ANSWER: (a) In the hallway. Then next most frequently in the classroom and then in the parking lot.

7. People can claim sexual harassment even if they have not been touched.

   ANSWER: TRUE. Making unwanted sexual comments or showing sexually explicit materials to someone who does not want them is sexual harassment.

8. Sexual harassment is against the law in 34 states and is now being considered in 12 others.

    ANSWER: FALSE. Sexual harassment is against federal laws which means they are effective in all 50 states. It is a third degree felony and is punishable by fines and/or jail time.

9. Sexual harassment is against school rules.

    ANSWER: TRUE. Not only is it against school rules, but most school districts have a written a policy against sexual harassment.

10. According to a national survey of middle and high school students, about 55% of all students have been sexually harassed.

    ANSWER: FALSE. Survey results showed that about 80% of school children experience some form of sexual harassment.

11. Sexual harassment can happen as early as Kindergarten although it happens for the first time most often in the middle school grades.

    ANSWER: TRUE.

12. Sexual harassment happens because when a person gets excited, he or she can't control himself or herself.

    ANSWER: FALSE. Sexual harassment happens because someone decided to act in a certain way.

13. Under the "new" laws, what used to be considered flirting is now known as sexual harassment.

    ANSWER: FALSE. Unwanted sexual attention has always been harassment and has been around for a very long time.

14. A husband cannot be found guilty of sexual harassment when it comes to his wife because they are married.

    ANSWER: FALSE. Having a marriage license does not give permission to treat your partner as a victim.

15. At least half the boys who are sexually harassed say that it was a girl who did it.

    ANSWER: TRUE. About 57% do.

16. Being at a party with alcohol increases the chances of sexual harassment happening.

    ANSWER: TRUE. Alcohol usually impairs a person's judgment and ability to make good decisions.

17. Victims of sexual harassment feel so bad that they often do not want to come to school.

    ANSWER: TRUE.

Now say ...   *Sexual harassment is unwanted and unwelcome sexual behavior which interferes with one's life. Sexual harassment is not behaviors that one likes or wants, such as kissing, touching, or flirting that is wanted. It is a topic that needs to be talked about. It is a problem in society that your generation will help solve. No longer can sexual harassment be ignored or tolerated. It is destructive to business, government, marriages, schools, and communities.*

Conclusion:

Finally say...   *You will have an opportunity to help bring about some changes in the way people relate to one another and to improve your own relationships. It may be one of most valuable topics that you will ever study.*

If there is anyone in our group who is uncomfortable or embarrassed about this topic, you may want to talk with me privately. In the meantime, unless I hear otherwise from you, we will meet again... and talk more specifically about the nature and extent of the problem of sexual harassment. Hope you enjoyed today's activity and I look forward to seeing you next week.

Session 2: **Sexual Harassment Mythology**

Objectives: To increase awareness of sexual harassment mythology; to confront false beliefs about sexual harassment.

Materials: Masking tape, large signs (see Session 2 Reproducibles, pp.156-160) for the corners of the room designating level of agreement.

Procedure: Before you get started, tape the levels of agreement signs (Strongly Agree, Agree, Strongly Disagree, and Disagree) in each corner of the room. The "Uncertain" sign should go somewhere in the center of the room. If the corners of the room are too far apart, you may not be able to manage the students as well as if the corners were closer together. If you have a large room, you may want to use tables instead.

First say... *Last week we took a look at some facts about sexual harassment. Our mission was to make sure that we had a clear picture of the problem. Today we will be looking at something similar—some of the myths surrounding our topic.*

Key Questions:

1. What is a myth?

    ANSWER: A myth is a story that is not true although it gets passed on as if it were true.

2. What might be a myth about boys?

    ANSWER: There are many. One might be that all boys always want sexual attention. This is not true. Some boys are annoyed and embarrassed by sexual attention.

3. What might be a myth about girls?

    ANSWER: There are also many myths about girls. One is that if a girl wants to be alone with you, then she wants sexual attention. This may not be true. There are many reasons why a girl would want to be alone with a boy including wanting to talk, study, or watch television.

Activity 2.1: Go to Your Corner!

First say...   *Sorting out the myths from the facts about sexual harassment can be difficult and confusing. We hear about things from people who really do not know the facts or who have been misinformed. Sometimes it is tricky. So, if you make a mistake, you're not alone.*

Then say...   *Let's play a game called Go To Your Corner! The way it works is that I will read a statement about sexual harassment. The statement could be a fact or it could be a myth. You will have to decide how much you agree or disagree with the statement. Your choices are Strongly Agree, Agree, Disagree, and Strongly Disagree. You will have time to think about it and then I will say "Go to your corner." Go to the corner of the room that has the appropriate sign. (Pause and show each sign.) For those of you who cannot make up your mind, you can go to the center of the room where it says "Uncertain."*

- After you read each statement and students have had a chance to go to their respective corners, instruct students on opposite sides (for instance, the Disagree and Agree corners or the Strongly Disagree and Strongly Agree corners) to talk about their decisions. They can try to persuade the other groups, including the "Uncertain" group, that their position is the "correct" one.

- After some discussion, have the undecided students think about the arguments they have heard, make a decision, and go to one of the four corners.

- Then, after you have regained their attention, provide the correct answers and rationale provided for you after each statement. Try to get through the first three. Others are provided in case you find that you have more time.

- Remember to save time at the end for closing statements.

Go to Your Corner!—Questions:

1. Some people like being sexually harassed.

    ANSWER: FALSE. Remember, sexual harassment is unwanted sexual attention. Nobody likes to be humiliated, embarrassed, and hurt. People who believe this do not understand the difference between sexual harassment and flirting.

2. When someone dresses in a "sexy" way, they deserve to be sexually harassed.

    ANSWER: FALSE. Nobody deserves to be humiliated, embarrassed, or hurt. This is what sexual harassment does. Dressing in a certain way could attract attention. People may be attracted and look. They may even approach the person. However, unwelcome behavior is still inappropriate and could constitute harassment.

3. A person who claims he or she is being sexually harassed simply needs to relax and see it as fun.

> **ANSWER: FALSE.** Sexual harassment is a crime. It is never, ever relaxing or fun. Believing this myth is as ridiculous as believing that, "If you are going to be hit in the head with a stick, then you might as well sit down and enjoy it."

4. People say that they don't want it, but they really do want sexual attention.

> **ANSWER: DEPENDS.** Every once in a while someone might say they don't want sexual attention when they really do. It may be too embarrassing for that person to actually admit it. Or, they may not want others to think anything negative of them. However, when we believe that someone really means "yes" when they are saying "no," then we are not listening to them. So, it is always much healthier to talk openly about it and find out for sure how a person really feels than to interpret, for yourself, what you think the person really means.

5. When it comes to sexual attention, sometimes "no" means "maybe."

> **ANSWER: FALSE.** A person might want to believe that a "no" means "maybe." This leaves room for opportunity. At the same time, however, this leaves room for terrible mistakes. Therefore, one must always take a "no" to mean "no." If the person who said "no" really meant "yes" then it is their problem and they will have to do something else to get what they want.

6. Many girls cry "sexual harassment" because they have sex with a boy and then they are embarrassed when someone else finds out.

> **ANSWER: FALSE.** This situation might happen every once in a while but it is rare. Maybe people think it happens more often than it does because when it does happen, it is usually told on national news and talked about a great deal.

- Instruct everyone to go back to their seats.

Discussion Questions:

1. What is one thing you learned today about sexual harassment?

2. How do myths about sexual harassment begin? How do they continue?

   ANSWER: Myths can begin in various ways. They can begin because people believe things even though they do not have any proof. These are called *assumptions*. They can begin as *stereotypes* (e.g., All boys want sexual attention). Myths can start just because a person is misinformed (e.g., Some people enjoy being sexually harassed). Myths about sexual harassment can be perpetuated by rumor and by the media such as television and movies.

3. Do your beliefs have an influence on how you act?

   ANSWER: Yes, what you believe influences how you act. For example, if you believed that all snakes are dangerous, you would not pick up a snake in front of you. Or, if you believed that studying for a test increases your chance of getting a good grade, you will be more motivated to study than if you believed that it did not help. This is important because if you were sold on a false belief about sexual harassment it could lead to trouble.

Conclusion:

Finally say... *Not everyone is in agreement about various beliefs concerning sexual harassment. You may have been surprised to discover that what you thought was true was really only a myth. This can happen to us as we continue to learn more about the world and mature. Since our beliefs influence how we behave, it is important to get the facts straight.*

During our next time together, we will continue learning more about what sexual harassment is and what it is not.

Session 3: **Is it Sexual Harassment?**

Objectives: To help students identify sexual harassment when it occurs.

Materials: Scenario Discussion Sheets (see Session 3 Reproducibles, pp. 161-163) to be handed to small group leaders.

Procedure:

Open by saying...   *As you know by now, sexual harassment has become a problem in society that affects the way in which people work together. This problem often begins early in life, especially during the middle school years.*

Now say...   *We have already discussed some facts and myths about sexual harassment. To prevent it from happening, we need to recognize it when we see it. Today, we will look at some situations or cases. Let's put our heads together and figure out what makes up sexual harassment. For our next activity, we will break into four groups or teams.*

Activity 3.1: Is it Sexual Harassment?

- Divide the large group into three small groups. Divide them by the row they are in or by having the students count off to three, making sure that the groups are balanced by gender. Have them sit together in one of three designated places in the room.
- Have each small group decide on who their group leader will be (allow only about 30 seconds for this).
- Quickly go around the room and confirm each small group leader.
- Give each group leader a "Scenario Discussion Sheet" which corresponds to the scenario that his or her group is reviewing (e.g., group #1 gets the discussion sheet for scenario #1). ONLY the small group leader should see the sheet. Explain that it will be his or her job to:
    - Make certain his or her small group is on task; he or she can read the scenario aloud while the group members read along.
    - Ask the questions on the Scenario Discussion Sheet.
    - Report to the rest of the class what happened in the process of discussing the questions in his or her small group.
- Pass out Scenario 1 to group 1, Scenario 2 to group 2, and Scenario 3 to group 3.

Now say... *The task of each small group is to discuss your scenario. Try to agree on whether the situation constitutes sexual harassment or not. Also, each team should try to answer the questions provided with the scenarios. Team 1 will work on scenario 1, Team 2 on scenario 2, and Team 3 will work on Scenario 3.*

- Give each team 5 to 6 minutes to complete their tasks. You can walk around the room to monitor their progress. When each team has completed the task or at the end of the allotted time, begin to discuss each scenario. Each team's small group leader should read the scenario and report on the team's decision. Then, prompt each small group leader to tell about the various factors that were considered and what happened in the process.

Discussion questions:

1. What happened when the group tried to agree?
2. What was one issue where almost everyone agreed?
3. What was one issue where there was a lot of disagreement?
4. How did the group's answers to the questions compare to the written answers on the leader's handout?

Scenario 1:

Brian and Joe, both in the same English class, make comments about what type of girls they like. One day Brian says to Joe, "I like `em with little round butts." Brian laughed as usual. Jill was a girl in the next row and heard the comments. She told them that she found such talk disgusting and asked them to stop. Both Brian and Joe apologized to Jill. The next day, Jill once again overheard Brian in a deliberately loud voice make a similar comment. Brian and Joe continued to ignore Jill's confrontations. Jill began to feel helpless and upset. She found it very difficult to concentrate in class.

Scenario 1 Questions:

1. Is this sexual harassment? Why?

    ANSWER: Yes, Brian and Joe are guilty of sexual harassment. Even though the comments may not be offensive to every person, they are offensive to Jill. Therefore, Brian and Joe are creating a "hostile environment" for Jill. A hostile environment is when a person makes a situation very difficult for someone else to concentrate, study, and ultimately make good grades. If Jill really thought the comments were funny and played along, the situation would not be considered sexual harassment.

2. What could Jill have done to make it stop?

    ANSWER: Most people would like to make the victim responsible by saying things like, "She should just walk away," or "It's not the boys' fault that she can't take a joke." However, responsibility for preventing sexual harassment relies on all people involved. It is never the victim's fault for being sexually harassed. One thing Jill could do is to file an official complaint with a teacher, counselor, administrator, or even the school resource officer.

    • If the students have trouble coming up with ideas...

You might say... *Most people would have trouble coming up with ideas for Jill to stop the vulgar comments made by Brian and Joe. The problem is that it is difficult to control someone else's behavior. That is why it is the harasser's responsibility to stop.*

3. How else might Brian and Joe respond to Jill's complaints?

    ANSWER: Brian and Joe are either being insensitive or forgetful in this case. They should have taken Jill very seriously the first time. Also, Brian and Joe could talk to Jill about her feelings.

4. In addition to being offensive to Jill, what else is wrong with comments such as the one Brian and Joe made?

    ANSWER: Even if Jill didn't care about comments (e.g., "I like `em with small butts"), there is still something wrong. Such comments reflect a certain attitude towards females. Many people who say things like that see women as objects.

Scenario 2:

Carl rides the bus to school and back home every day. Just for fun, he wrote a note to Juanita and passed it to her. The note read, "You have a really nice body. How about you and I get together? Come over tonight!." After Juanita read the note and looked up at Carl, he made some sexual gestures with his hands, eyebrows, and lips.

Scenario 2 Questions

1. Is this sexual harassment? Why?

    ANSWER: MAYBE. It depends on whether Juanita is receptive to Carl's remarks or not. If Juanita enjoys this kind of attention, then it would not be sexual harassment. But if she found the remarks to be offensive and if Carl would not stop, then it would be considered sexual harassment. This type of sexual harassment would be considered visual, the most obvious and recognized. Carl may assume that such behavior is O.K. with Juanita and risk hurting her feelings.

2. How might Juanita have felt if Carl's behavior was unwanted?

    ANSWER: Juanita had no part in Carl's decision to pass the offensive note or make the offensive gestures. She may have felt various unpleasant feelings including invaded, helpless, angry, or embarrassed. No one should be made to feel this way. Such unpleasant experiences can negatively affect Juanita's academic performance, social confidence, and self-esteem.

3. Why might Carl have acted this way?

    ANSWER: All sorts of reasons, none of which excuse his behavior. Carl may believe that such behavior is harmless. He may have wanted some type of attention and did not know of a better way of getting it. Carl also might have done it because it makes him feel playful, although at Juanita's expense. Some people, maybe even Carl, believe that girls enjoy that kind of attention, even against their will. Finally, he may simply be mean spirited and enjoys creating discomfort and even agony in others. Remember, these might be explanations for Carl's behavior but certainly not excuses. There is no justification for sexual harassment.

Scenario 3:

A group of four girls frequently whistle "wolf calls" at Jamal. Jamal thought it was kind of neat and enjoyed the special attention. After a while, when the girls didn't stop, Jamal began to feel embarrassed and uncomfortable. He no longer considered the attention special and began to feel upset. He told them to quit but they would laugh and continue. Jamal didn't really know what to do. Jamal just wanted to be left alone.

Scenario 3 Questions:

1. Is this sexual harassment? Why?

    ANSWER: At first Jamal enjoyed the wolf calls and probably wanted the girls to continue. However, there came a time when it was no longer fun and he wanted it to stop. The point at which he did not consent to the wolf calls and told the girls was the moment sexual harassment began.

2. Do boys really experience sexual harassment?

    ANSWER: Yes. Sexual harassment for a male can be just as unpleasant as it is for a female.

3. What might the girls have thought about Jamal's request for them to stop whistling at him? Why?

    ANSWER: Many people buy into the myth that boys are always ready and willing when it comes to sexual attention. It's simply not true. Boys are not always "turned on" by sexual attention. Boys may prefer to be left alone. The sad thing is that when a male refuses sexual attention, others may inappropriately label him as "less of a boy or man."

4. What might some of the other boys think if they knew that Jamal told the girls to stop whistling?

    ANSWER: The other boys may tease Jamal saying that he should enjoy it or to say something "sexy" back to them.

* Have the students stay in their groups while you make some concluding comments.

Discussion Questions:

1. What is one thing that you learned today about sexual harassment?

2. What are some examples of sexual harassment that takes place in school?

   ANSWER: Examples of sexual harassment include making comments about a person's body or a part of their body; making sexually explicit material such as posters, pictures, or handmade drawings public; making academic achievement a condition of sexual favors; or spreading rumors of a sexual nature about a person.

3. How can sexual harassment influence production in school? On the job?

   ANSWER: Sexual harassment can seriously lessen performance on the job or at school. It is very difficult to work when you are feeling embarrassed, angry, degraded, humiliated, and disgusted. Sexual harassment also instills fear and can make the person think less of themselves.

4. What makes the business world concerned about this problem?

   ANSWER: Sexual harassment decreases productivity which means loss of money. It kills team work and is against the law. A company can be sued for a lot of money if they allow sexual harassment to occur.

Conclusion:

Conclude with... *We practiced recognizing sexual harassment. It is also important to do our part in not letting it happen to us or others. This involves several skills which we will examine when we meet again.*

Next time we are going to think more about how we might be more attentive to each other so that we do not miss out on what the other is trying to say.

Session 4: **The Web**

Objectives: To teach how sexual harassment has both a direct and indirect impact on others. To promote self-disclosure about topics related to healthy and mutually respectful relationships.

Materials: One ball of yarn.

Procedure:

First say...   *So far, we have discussed some facts about sexual harassment including it's definition. Remember that sexual harassment is unwanted sexual attention that interferes with your life. We also talked about myths. Further, we discussed different types of situations and whether they were cases of sexual harassment or not.*

Then say...   *The impact of this social problem is far reaching. You and I may be affected by others who engage in sexual harassment whether we realize it or not. Today you will have a chance to say more about what is on your mind concerning this social problem.*

Activity 4.1: The Spider Web

- Have your group first form a circle for a go-around discussion. They can either stand or sit, whichever is most comfortable and appropriate.

Now say...   *I'm going to ask some questions and give a few topics to discuss in our group. Here are the basic guidelines:*

1. To contribute to the discussion, you must have in your possession this ball of yarn. The first person holds the yarn, shares their comments, and passes the ball to the next person who wants to speak. The next person holds the yarn before passing it to someone else who wants to speak. You can only speak when you have the ball of yarn. The person who has the ball of yarn chooses who to pass it to next. This continues until the discussion ends.

2. The first student to talk holds the end piece of a ball of yarn. He or she begins the discussion and passes it to the next speaker. Remember to leave about 10 minutes at the end for processing.

3. Have one person volunteer to start the discussion.

The following questions can be used for the group discussion:

1. Some people say that love is how you feel and others say that love is an action. What do you think the meaning of love is?

2. Everyone needs to feel like they have some personal power. Some people do this through sexual harassment, which is destructive. How can you feel powerful without being destructive?

3. If you could be invisible for 10 minutes, any time during the day or night, how would you use the power? Is this ethical? Legal? Moral?

   - After some time, a pattern will evolve with the string that looks like a spider web. The pattern is a type of histogram which reflects the order in which members of the group spoke. The shape of the web also reveals dynamics about the group. Group members who are more comfortable with each other usually create a more intricate pattern than groups with lower levels of trust and comfort. A group that has members who are not very trustworthy of each other will create more of a circle of string with a big hole in the middle. This is because when members of a group experience a low level of comfort (i.e., they do not experience the facilitative conditions), they usually just pass the yarn to the person right next to them.

   - After the web of yarn begins to evolve, most every time, students will start "tugging" on their piece so as to affect the whole web. They will usually laugh while watching how they can send vibrations throughout the web. It can be used as an analogy for how sexual harassment has a direct and indirect affect on our society.

   - Have the students look closely at the web. They might all lift it high on the count of three and look at it from below. While holding the web, use the following discussion questions to process the activity.

Discussion Questions:

1. What can we say about our group based on the design of our spider web?

2. If one part of the string moves, what happens to the rest of the web? How is this related to people's actions or words?

3. If the group feels "together," what has made it this way? If people in our group still do not trust others, what can each of us do for that to enhance more trust?

4. How did one person's contribution to the discussion affect what followed?

5. How would you describe a time when your actions or words had an impact on someone else and you didn't find out until later that this happened?

6. How might sexual harassment affect us even if we have not experienced it directly?

Note: When sexual harassment happens in business and schools, it disrupts the working environment. For individuals, it decreases their productivity because it is difficult to get work done when you feel angry, helpless, humiliated, or hurt. Sometimes an employee resigns which forces the employer to hire and train someone new. This costs money. These extra costs are passed on to the consumer—people like you and I who purchase products and services. Some other ways that sexual harassment can affect you is that 1) it makes people not trust others; 2) it creates a insecure learning environment at school; 3) drains resources that could be used in more useful areas; and 4) models destructive behavior for others.

Now say... *Thank you for your contributions to our discussion and our work of art (point to the web). Together we have worked together to learn about how peoples' behavior, especially when it involves sexual harassment, can spread even when we are not directly involved. I especially appreciate all your ideas and input during our conversation.*

Session 5: **What are You Trying to Say?**

Objectives: To teach communication skills which include active listening and nonverbal communication.

Materials: You GIZZYDEECH Cards, The Blind Spot Paragraph (see Session 5 Reproducibles, pp. 164-165).

Procedure:

First say... *This is our fifth session together and we will want to make the best use of our time. You probably remember that last week, we discussed different types of situations and whether they were cases of sexual harassment.*

Then say... *Sometimes we ignore other person's words and feelings. Being a careful listener is both an art and a science. Have you ever noticed how some people are good listeners, when others seem to be distracted and have trouble paying attention? Some people are tuned into what you are feeling and thinking, whereas others are not. Being a good communicator and problem-solver relies on being an attentive listener.*

Now say... *Today, we are going to look at some ways in which you can become a better listener. As a person is talking, try to listen carefully for both pleasant and unpleasant feelings. Ask yourself: "What is the person experiencing in the situation?" Can you say aloud the feelings you are hearing? Let's listen to a few examples:*

Activity 5.1: You Gizzydeech!

- Have the students volunteer to help by raising their hands.
- Then, choose ten of these students balanced for gender and race.
- Take them aside and give them each a "You Gizzydeech" card. Make sure they can all pronounce the word.
- In turn, have the students, in front of the class, read aloud the sentences they have on their cards. They should read the sentence and focus on the feeling indicated on the card. They can also use their hands and facial expressions. Each card should result in a different tone of voice and body language.
- After each student reads a card, have the students try to guess the feeling being expressed. This game is similar to charades.
- The "You Gizzydeech" cards include the following:

> Read with excitement: "You are such a Gizzydeech."
>
> Read with sadness: "You are such a Gizzydeech."
>
> Read with anger: "You are such a Gizzydeech."
>
> Read with pride: "You are such a Gizzydeech."
>
> Read with fear: "You are such a Gizzydeech."
>
> Read with NO feeling: "You are such a Gizzydeech."
>
> Read with surprise: "You are such a Gizzydeech."
>
> Read with depression: "You are such a Gizzydeech."
>
> Read with confusion: "You are such a Gizzydeech."
>
> Read with love: "You are such a Gizzydeech."

Discussion Questions:

1. What might the word Gizzydeech mean?

   ANSWER: Actually, the word doesn't mean anything, it was made up.

2. How did you know what feeling was being expressed without knowing the meaning of the word Gizzydeech?

   ANSWER: Perhaps you might have been able to tell the meaning of the word by the speaker's feeling and expressions.

3. How might it feel for someone not to know what you are trying to say?

   ANSWER: It probably feels frustrating. You may even feel helpless or left out.

4. Could the same statements have different meanings based on how they are said?

    ANSWER: Yes indeed. Peoples' tone of voice and their expressions can change the meaning of what is said.

5. When someone says something but that person's body "says something else," which do you believe?

    ANSWER: Most of the time, the listener will find that a person's body language is the most accurate. This is because the speaker cannot influence body motions as well as they can the words. However, it can still be difficult to interpret, even confusing. When in doubt, an individual should always ask what the other person is trying to say or is feeling.

6. How does attitude affect what a person actually hears?

    ANSWER: You may have heard that "people hear what they want to hear." There is a great deal of truth to this statement. What people want (or need) to hear may influence the meaning they place on what is actually said. When listening to others, it is always important to keep our own prejudices aside and listen with an open mind. Misinterpreting what someone says can lead to trouble.

Now say...   *Our volunteers have demonstrated how the same word, which in this case does not mean anything, can give a different message just by how it is said. You noticed that each person was saying the sentence with a different feeling and with different expressions. People can say a great deal with just body language.*

Finally say...   *To be effective communicators, people need to be receptive and open to others' words, feelings, and actions. Being an effective listener is hard work; yet, it is necessary for healthy and happy relationships.*

Activity 5.2: The Blind Spot

Open by saying... *We have talked about body language and how it plays an important part in communication. Now let's turn to a different activity that should give us some further insight into what it means to be in tune to the messages that we get through our eyes and ears.*

- Pass out the "Blind Spot" sheet (see Session Reproducibles). Make sure that the students put them face down and do NOT read them until you say so.

Now say... *Okay, In a few moments we will be reading together what is written on the sheets of paper that was just passed out. Then, I will give you a very quick task that should only last a few seconds so you'll have to be on your toes. Are you ready? OK, turn your papers over....*

- Have the students turn the papers over and have everyone read aloud. The paragraph contains the following:

    "One of the best feelings is the feeling of love. If a person is a special friend of yours, that is also a kind of love. Feelings of fear may come with love."

- Instruct the students to quickly count the number of letter F's in the sentence. Give them about 15 seconds.

Discussion Questions:

1. How many letter F's did you count?

    ANSWER: There are actually eleven in the sentence although most people will probably not count them all.

2. How come there are different answers even though everyone has the same paper?

    ANSWER: The reason is that most people miss the F's in the word "of" because it sounds more like a "v" than an "f."

3. What might you have learned about communication from this exercise?

    ANSWER: This exercise attempts to show that communication is not always easy. We must work hard to make sure that we hear and see everything that is intended. The best way to do this is to listen carefully to words and feelings, confirm, and ask questions.

Russell A. Sabella, Ph.D. & Robert D. Myrick, Ph.D.

4. Is it possible that you can be wrong about something even though you think that you are absolutely right?

ANSWER: Yes, that is why we should put off getting defensive and try to learn.

Now say... *Our exercise showed us how we all have what is called a blind spot. Many times we just do not see things that are right in front of us. In a similar way, we do not always hear things that are spoken directly to us either. In these cases, we must try to get help from others to help us see or hear things in our blind spot. For example, in this situation, rather than arguing about how many letter F's there are in the paragraph, we could ask others to show us how they arrived at their answer.*

Conclusion:

Finally say... *In relationships we must be careful to hear the other person's words and feelings. If we do not, then we might miss something important which could eventually lead to hurt feelings.*

In our next session, we will look at the importance of mutual respect. See you next week!

Session 6: **Hey! You're in My Space!**

Objectives: To teach the concept of people's comfort zone.

Materials: Party Game Labels (see Session 6 Reproducibles, pp. 166-169), tape, a radio or tape player (optional)

Open by saying... *The last time we met we learned more about what it means to be an attentive listener. We played the Gizzydeech game and also talked about blind spots. We found that it takes lots of work to really understand what someone is saying and feeling. We also discussed how important it is to be an attentive listener to prevent hurting a person's feelings.*

Then say... *Today we are going to talk about respect. Respect is an expression of consideration, especially for a person's feelings. Respect is also showing appreciation. What does the word respect mean to you? What are other ways that people are shown respect? Let's find out ....*

Activity 6.1: The Party

First say... *It's time for our next activity. Let's begin by using a little imagination. At this time, let's have a party. Our party will be somewhat different, however, because each person will have a different set of instructions to follow. Each of you will receive a piece of paper taped on his or her back. The paper will have a message telling others how to act with you.*

Then say... *After everyone gets his or her paper, I will give you some topics to discuss as you talk and get to know each other. Between each topic I will say "STOP." At that time, please turn your attention to me for the next topic. As you discuss the topics, others may react to your special message. Oh yes, do not share the personal messages with anyone until the party is over! Later on we will see if the persons wearing a message can guess what it is.*

Russell A. Sabella, Ph.D. & Robert D. Myrick, Ph.D.

- Tape a message to each of student's back. Some students will receive the same message. The messages include:
    - Disregard the topic and make comments about my feet! Say things like, "Ooooh, those are the best looking pair of feet I have ever seen!"
    - Disregard the topic and make comments about my hands! Say things like, "Ooooh, those are the best looking pair of hands I have ever seen!"
    - I hate it when people look me directly in the eyes when talking with me.
    - I might be interested in going together with you.
    - I like to talk with others ONLY when there is nobody around.
    - I like people to get up close to me when I'm talking with them.
    - I scare you. Act nervous when talking to me.
    - I am not comfortable with people "in my face." Stay at least 5 feet away when talking to me.
    - You find me attractive.
    - You are VERY interested in getting my phone number.
    - You are extremely interested in what I have to say.
- If you have a cassette or CD player, begin playing some party music loud enough to hear but not too loud as to disturb any neighbors. If not, that's OK too, just skip this part. Then start the party by reading the first topic. After about two minutes, say STOP, wait to get their attention, and read the next topic. Here are the topics to use:
- How would you describe the last party you were at?
- What is your favorite thing to do on the weekend when you don't have any chores or other responsibilities?
-
    If you had to choose a favorite musician or musical group, who would it be and why?
- If someone gave you a million dollars to throw the next party, on the condition that you spent every dollar on the party, how would you do it?
- Ask the following questions:
    1. How did other people behave towards you?
    2. What do you think your personal message says?

Follow up Discussion and Questions:

1. How was communication affected by your message?

   ANSWER: How people see you or how they think of you will affect how they speak with you.

2. How did you know when you were too close or too far from the person with whom you are speaking?

   ANSWER: You must judge by the person's expressions to know if they are comfortable with you. This can be difficult and, therefore, the person must be willing to communicate their comfort level.

3. What is a person's comfort zone?

   ANSWER: It is the amount of space around you, at any given time or situation, that you feel comfortable with someone else.

4. How is a person's comfort zone a consideration in sexual harassment?

   ANSWER: Repeatedly invading a person's comfort zone (that is, getting too close) and making them uncomfortable with sexual attention is considered sexual harassment.

Now say... *You have all had a chance to interact at our special party. The goal of this particular activity was to teach the idea of people's comfort zone. Each person brings to a conversation many things: ideas, beliefs, habits, skills, and a comfort zone. Some of you experienced what it was like trying to figure out how to get into a comfortable stance for both you and the other person with whom you were talking. If someone was closer to you than you wanted, you might have felt annoyed. When someone gives you unwanted sexual attention, in the form of words, pictures, or actions, the feelings only get stronger. You might feel angry, confused, helpless, and even violated. It is important to make certain that the other person is interested and open to your comments or behavior no matter what the nature of your conversation is about.*

Conclude by saying... *We are winding down with our time. Next week we will explore and try to further understand the nature of sexual harassment. We will take a look at how to reduce the risk of it happening and discuss how to best help our friends if it happens to them.*

Session 7: **Helping Yourself and Others**

Objectives: To teach students how to confront a perpetrator; report sexual harassment; effectively support and help others experiencing sexual harassment.

Materials: "Memo" Handout, "Helping a Friend Who Has Been Sexually Harassed" Handout, "Options for Confronting Sexual Harassment" Handout, and an "Options for Confronting Sexual Harassment" Handout cut in strips (see Session 7 Reproducibles, pp. 170-172).

Activity 7.1: Opt to STOP!

First say...   *"Since our first session, we have discussed the definition of sexual harassment, some related myths, how to recognize it when you see it happening, and the importance of respecting a person's comfort zone. Now we must turn to the topic of what you might do to confront sexual harassment if it happens to you or a friend.*

Then say...   *Let us look at some options that you might have for stopping sexual harassment. Options gives you the power to choose. Although you may not have the power to control the behavior of the perpetrator, you do have the power to stand up for your rights and get help.*

Now ask...   *What might be some options for confronting sexual harassment when you see it? Remember that violence is not an acceptable option.*

- After brainstorming for about three to four minutes, pass out the handout called "Options for Confronting Sexual Harassment"
- Point out the options that students were able to offer. Then, point out the options that they did or did not mention. When you get to Option 6, pass out the "Memo" handout.

Say...   *This handout will guide you in writing an official notification of your sexual harassment experience. You can send it to any adult that you trust.*

Now ask...   *Are there any other options for confronting sexual harassment that we missed?*

Now say...   *Okay, confronting a perpetrator of sexual harassment is a skill. Like any skill, to get good at it, you have to practice. I need everyone to bring your chairs into a circle around the room. (If the structure of your room does not allow it, then, have students stand in a circle).*

- Put an empty chair in the middle of the circle.

Then say...   *Now that you are all in a circle, let me explain what comes next. Each person will pick from a box one option for confronting sexual harassment. Pretending that the perpetrator is sitting in the chair in the middle of the circle, use the option you picked to confront him/her. You can make up what you think the perpetrator did in your personal confrontation.*

- Begin the activity by letting a volunteer pick out of the box and practicing that option. If students are somewhat hesitant, you might want to begin yourself.
- If at any time a student does not want to participate, allow him or her to pass. If a student passes, come back to him or her after everyone who wants a turn has had one and ask if he or she would like to try it now.
- Remember to offer a few complimentary words as you go along to encourage participation and reinforce skillful confrontations.
- After the last person has had a turn...

Say...   *Terrific! Just remember that you have the right to not have anyone victimize you with sexual harassment. If someone does, you can use any or all of these options to confront him/her. You also have the choice to go right to option 6 and make an official complaint. If you can, always seek the help of your parents/guardians. Now let's turn to the most effective way to help and support a friend who has been sexually harassed.*

Russell A. Sabella, Ph.D. & Robert D. Myrick, Ph.D.

Activity 7.2: Helping a Friend Who Has Been Sexually Harassed

First say...   *What can you do to help a friend who is experiencing sexual harassment feel supported? (Pause for answers.) One way is to make sure that you do NOT blame him or her in any way for the harassment. For example, you do not want to say that he or she should have expected the harassment because of what he or she was wearing or what was said.*

Then say...   *Let's take a look at some other things you can do to help a friend who is suffering from sexual harassment.*

- Pass out the Helping a Friend Who Has Been Sexually Harassed handout (see Session Reproducibles).
- Review the handout with the students. Point out the items that they were able to say and those that they did not.
- Finally, bring attention to the section with resource numbers in case they need to use them.

Key Questions:

1. Is it possible that someone you know would do something that could be considered sexual harassment?

   ANSWER: Yes. It is difficult to believe that someone you know would harass someone but it could be true. This person may be just as guilty of sexual harassment as a stranger. This doesn't mean that you should not be friends with this person. What it does mean is that you have an obligation to help your friend stop the harassment before he or she hurts anyone else.

2. What is the difference between an informal and a formal complaint?

   ANSWER: An informal complaint is made unofficially. That is, the complaint is not written. A formal complaint follows certain guidelines and always involves a written description of the incident(s). Formal complaints are needed to make a legal case against the harasser if informal efforts are not successful.

3. What if sexual harassment happens with an adult?

ANSWER: This is an especially tough situation because adults are supposed to know better, be responsible, and trustworthy. Even though this is ideal, the truth is that not all adults are trustworthy. Therefore, a young person who experiences sexual harassment by an adult should follow the same guidelines for when a student is the harasser. The adult harasser needs to be confronted and stopped.

Conclusion:

Finally say... *Take what you've learned to help fight sexual harassment. Only when we all do our part will sexual harassment become a thing of the past. We hope that you've also enjoyed our time together. If you have any other questions about sexual harassment, remember that you have many caring and knowledgeable adults around who can help. All you have to do is talk with them.*

Session 8: Moving Around and Moving Ahead

Objectives: To evaluate student outcomes; to help students make a future commitment towards preventing sexual harassment.

Materials:
Large pieces of paper
Pencils and crayons
Sexual Harassment Inventory (see Figure 8.1, pp. 145-146)
School Atmosphere Inventory (see Figure 8.2, p. 147)
Sexual Harassment Unit Evaluation (see Figure 8.3, p. 148)
Contract (Optional) (see Session 8 Reproducible, p. 172)
Certificate of Completion (Optional) (see Session 8 Reproducible, p. 173)

Procedure:

First say... *The activities and discussions about sexual harassment were designed to make you become more aware of this national problem. It was to help you clarify issues and think of ways in which it might be resolved and prevented. This unit, of course, was based on the assumption that things would be better for all of us if we treated one another with more respect and kindness.*

Then say... *Let's think what we have done and evaluate our efforts. What have we learned? Or, relearned? What else might we have done, or done differently? Where do we go from here?*

Activity 8.1: I Learned

Ask each person in the room to complete the following four questions on his or her paper:

1. What was your favorite activity or discussion during our time together? Why?
2. What is one thing you learned about sexual harassment?
3. What is one thing that you now want to say about sexual harassment that you did not have a chance to say before?
4. What is one way that you could personally take a stand against sexual harassment?

Now say... *Let's divide into some smaller groups so that we can move more easily from one station to another.*

Point to each of the four stations in the room, which will have a chart or long piece of paper where students can record their responses. Then, teams are assigned to one of the four stations and given a few minutes to draw pictures, symbols or use phrases to represent their response to the question posed at that position. For example, at station #1 (Favorite Activity), all students use pencils and crayons to record their response. They can sign with their initials.

On a signal given by the leader, teams rotate to the next stations (e.g., One Thing Learned; One More Comment; A Next Step) and make their recordings.

These four papers are posted on the wall and discussed. Clarifications are requested and additional comments are solicited. Themes are identified.

If time permits, the large group is then assembled for any final evaluations. Students then complete the Sexual Harassment Inventory (Figure 8.1) as a post evaluation. The School Atmosphere Inventory (Figure 8.2) might also be included. A unit evaluation may also take place (Figure 8.3).

If time permits, a final go-around might also be appropriate in which each student makes a final statement about the problem, their concern, or their concluding thought.

Optional: A copy of the Contract (see Session Reproducibles) is passed around the room and each group member signs it.

Optional: The Certificate of Completion (see Session Reproducibles) can be given to each group member, or it might be shown on a classroom screen using a transparency and overhead projector. You might then say, "Congratulations. This was a difficult topic that required you to be mature and to look at a problem that affects society, especially the one that you and your peers will help build in the future. Changes can be for better or for worse. Your help in preventing sexual harassment and other forms of victimizing people can make a positive difference in building a better world. Thanks for your cooperation, sharing your ideas, and taking part in the activities."

Conclusion:

Now say... *Sexual harassment is any unwanted sexual attention that interferes with your life. You have a right to be treated with dignity. Preventing sexual harassment is a worthwhile goal in which everyone can be involved. Through both words and actions, personal rights will be protected and enhanced. You can help create a better society, one in which everyone will feel safe and respected.*

Russell A. Sabella, Ph.D. & Robert D. Myrick, Ph.D.

Supplemental Activities

The Guidance Unit described earlier was designed as a series of activities and dialogues to focus attention on the issues related to sexual harassment. Sometimes, a teacher or group facilitator may want to extend a discussion through another activity. On other occasions, it is possible to substitute an activity in the unit with another, keeping in mind the basic objectives of a session and how it is tied to the goals of the unit.

Supplemental group activities provide an opportunity to further explore particular issues or perhaps to examine certain elements related to harassment. The activities may elicit a discussion of human feelings and behaviors, as well as appropriate and inappropriate social practices. It is the facilitator's task to link the activity, which is only a tool or vehicle, to any relevant questions to be discussed. In the case of sexual harassment, an activity is worthwhile if it helps participants examine human nature and to look for social alternatives that show respect for others.

Dear Abby

In this activity, the leader begins by saying, "I want you to think of a problem that has involved sexual harassment or some other inappropriate behavior. This may be something that was done to you or someone else. It is a problem moment. Write a Dear Abby letter, explaining the situation or problem, perhaps what you saw or heard. Don't sign your name. By the way, I have some more that have been given to me by other students and I'll include those in our collection." (Give time for students to write a problem). "Now, let me collect your Dear Abby notes."

In this case, the leader keeps and reads aloud the problems. After reading the problem, and making appropriate editing changes that will both protect the writer and facilitate discussion, the leader selects one at a time and reads it aloud.

One general procedure is to have a panel of about four to five students from the group sit in front of the room and react to the problem that is presented to them. Then, others in the room are encouraged to add their comments. Three or four panel groups are rotated after discussing two issues each, giving everyone in the large group an opportunity to participate.

Or, another procedure is to take the problems, include a few more, and have them typed on strips of paper. Then, divide the large group into four or five smaller groups, giving each two or three slips for discussion. Groups select one of the problems that they discussed to talk about with the whole class.

Here are some sample problems that may be included in with the group's contribution.

- I like a girl, but I don't know what to say to let her know that I really like her. She might take what I say the wrong way.

- Some guys were talking about the physical appearance of a girl who I think is kinda cool. They make jokes about her having sex with a lot of boys. I'm not sure what to say or do when they talk that way?

- Once I was with a group of guys when a girl walked by. One of the guys pretended like he was going to put his hands on her breasts and wiggled his fingers. The boys laughed. The girl walked on. What should I have said or done?

- I like my friends. But sometimes when a girl walks by in the hallway at school, they start making noises and harassing her. They don't really mean anything by it. They're just teasing, but I don't want to get in trouble.

- I know a girl who enjoys teasing boys by the way she dresses and the things that she says to them. She's just asking for trouble. But, she thinks its cool if they get all hot and bothered by her.

- A friend of mine is being harassed. Her name and telephone number are written on the boy's bathroom wall, along with a bunch of crude things about her. None of it is true, but she doesn't know what to do.

The facilitator, or group leader, will focus on 1) feelings (pleasant and unpleasant) of the people associated with the problem; 2) possible behaviors or actions that are related to those feelings; 3) some possible solutions. You might ask, "How would you feel if this were your problem?" "How do you think the person who is being harassed is feeling?" If one feels that way, then how do you think he or she might act? What would you do, if this were your problem?

A Public Survey

Participants discuss the problem of sexual harassment and identify the significant issues. Then, working as a team of co- interviewers, they use open-ended questions to survey a population. The population may be adults or student groups. Then some comparisons are made between groups. Or, the group might put together their own set of survey questions, using a Likert-type scale to record answers by respondents (i.e., Strongly Agree, Agree, Uncertain, Disagree, Strongly Disagree).

Monkey See, Monkey Do

In this activity group participants write their names on a slip of paper. The names are collected and put into a paper bag or some other kind of container. One person picks a name from the bag and, without revealing the name, begins to mimic the behavior or actions of the person whose name was on the piece of paper. Every attempt is made to feel and behave like the person, without giving away the name. At the end of the time period, members try to guess who was copying or playing whom.

Discuss how some people learn to mimic other people's behaviors? Is this done consciously or unconsciously, or both? Which behaviors are mimicked most by teenagers? What makes some of those behaviors so desired? How much of what we do in life is mimicking of others? Is there any freedom of choice in how we act around others?

Try to Escape

A volunteer agrees to enter the center of a circle of group members. The person is then told to "try to escape" or break out of the enclosure, as others in the outer circle hold each other's waists tightly. The circle is a strong chain which is difficult to break. Four or five people might try. After the member succeeds or ceases his or her efforts, another person is given a turn. Finally, the experience is discussed. What feelings did the volunteers have? What did they do to break out? What happened when it became increasingly difficult or if the group prevented a break out? To the group members: How did it feel to keep the person contained? Did you want the person to escape? If yes, why? If not, why not? What behaviors did you notice from the volunteers and from the group?

Finally, how is this related to someone who is trying to escape from being sexually harassed? How are the feelings and behaviors similar? Would the solutions be similar (e.g., politely asking to be let out)? Also, how is this related to someone who is trying to break away from a group's undesirable behavior?

Unfinished Sentences

Each member of the group is asked to write a response that completes the following unfinished sentences.

1. Girls should....
2. Boys should....
3. One of the things I like best about boys is....
4. One of the things I like best about girls is....
5. Sexual harassment is....
6. Being a boy is....
7. Being a girl is....
8. Being sexually harassed in school....
9. I get angry when someone....
10. I feel most appreciated when someone....

After everyone has finished, the groups discuss the experience. In particular, attention is given to items 5, 8, and 10.

The Dating Ritual

The group is invited to create new rituals for dating. After dividing into small groups, each group is given one of the following dating rituals to work into a skit that helps define how one acts and what one says in a dating situation. After a few minutes, each group then acts out their skit and group members try to guess the meaning of the rituals.

Rituals:

1. Crowing like a rooster
2. Hopping on one foot
3. Blinking five times
4. Putting the little finger in an ear
5. Patting one's head and stomach at the same time
6. Flapping arms like a big bird

During the discussion, the group is encouraged to think of how dating rituals can be confusing, as well as helpful. Rituals are related to interpersonal communication and social customs. What makes some behavior become a ritual while others are rejected or even considered taboo? Does our society need new customs when it comes to dating? Or, new ways of showing a positive interest in someone?

Another variation is to assign each of the rituals to a different group. Then, members of the different groups mill around the room using their new found ritual to communicate with others.

Still, another variation is that group participants draw at random slips of paper with one of the rituals. Then, the entire group mills around trying to find someone who is displaying a similar dating ritual. Did anyone feel harassed? Did it make a difference to find someone who had a similar ritual? How is this related to contemporary dating rituals? To sexual harassment?

The Graffiti Wall

There once was a large cement wall that was used to retain a small pond. The wall kept the water from flooding nearby streets and houses. It also provided an interesting place where people could write graffiti or any well wishes or messages that they might want to express. Almost everyone in the city seemed to enjoy looking at the colorful wall and reading things that were written there. Imagine that one day you were passing by and you noticed that three teenagers were writing inflammatory words that expressed their bigotry and prejudice toward a minority group. They laughed when they saw you and said it was "Just for fun!" But, you knew that the words were offensive to many people. What would you do?

   a. Would you discuss the matter with a friend?

   b. Would you tell the teenagers to stop?

   c. Would you discuss it with other people?

   d. Would you report it to a police officer who was on the corner of the street?

   e. What if they continued after being told to stop by the officer?

   f. Would it had made any difference if they had gone beyond writing, but were breaking down parts of the wall?

   g. What is the difference between harmless, playful graffiti and that which is derogatory and inappropriate?

   h. What action should be taken?

Lead a discussion about the graffiti wall before relating this incident with sexual harassment. Suppose that the issue had involved the harassment of someone (e.g., writing lewd messages of a sexual nature).

Russell A. Sabella, Ph.D. & Robert D. Myrick, Ph.D.

To Catch a Thief

Imagine that you are a member of a police force that has been asked to catch a thief who has been stealing important papers and documents, as well as jewelry and money from a well- respected person. The person says that the money is not as important as some of the jewelry, which consisted of heirloom rings and pins that had been passed down through the family. Their value was beyond actual monetary worth. In addition, there is a suspect who is being brought in for questioning, as well as someone who claims to have seen the suspect committing the robbery. What questions would you ask the suspect to help determine guilt or innocence? Make a list of the questions. Then, make another list of questions that you would ask the person who claims to have seen the suspect commit the crime.

In a discussion, examine the questions for those that help best in the investigation (facts and opinions). Then, ask the group members if they have ever been robbed. Do they know anyone who has been robbed or been a victim of a crime? If so, what were that person's feelings and how did they act?

Finally, ask the group if sexual harassment is in a sense a robbery? Does it rob a person of dignity? Does it take away their worth? Do they have similar feelings to people who have had things stolen from them? Is it a matter of fact or opinion? One robber invades a person's property and the harasser invades a person's personal space. How might it be the same or different?

Reporting a Murder

Suppose that you had witnessed a murder. You tell the police at the scene of the crime what you saw. Later, some of your friends say that you should mind your own business and not get involved. You now have been asked to come to the police station in order to give a full statement and account to the police of what you saw and heard. Will you:

1. Tell them you could not really see very well and were only guessing at some things.
2. Tell exactly what you saw and heard.
3. Tell them you won't talk and do not want to be involved for fear of being hunted and hurt by the murderer.
4. Tell a few things but be vague about it, so that you could later back away from the incident.
5. Change your story and say you didn't see anything.

Now imagine that a close friend was in a similar situation and asked for your opinion. Write a letter explaining your position and make a recommendation to your friend.

Next, relate this situation to that of seeing someone who is being sexually harassed in school. You have always tried to stay away from this group, knowing that they can be mean and vindictive. But, you witnessed harassment and the perpetrators have been called to the office. The victim is there and looks to you for help. What will you say? What would you advise others to do? How is what is happening to this victim different from victims in other situations? How might it be the same?

Russell A. Sabella, Ph.D. & Robert D. Myrick, Ph.D.

The Mystery Person

Write the following phrases on pieces of paper, which are then placed in an open container. Write the names of the following victims on the board. Have the group try to guess who is the Mystery Person, based on the clues read aloud.

Persons

Mr. Jones, a wealthy banker

Mrs. James, a successful stock broker

Mr. Anderson, a thief and burglar

Mrs. Ashton, a woman on an automobile assembly line who is being sexually harassed by a colleague at work

Mr. Bills, a police investigator

Clues

1. I love my work.
2. I try to avoid jumping to conclusions.
3. I am overly cautious and worry about what could happen next.
4. I sometimes fear that things can get worse and that I could be harmed.
5. I worry about my future.
6. I am afraid that others don't like me.
7. I am paranoid and suspect others of thinking harmful things.

Ask the group to make guesses as you move through the clues. Then, break into smaller groups, with each group given the task of coming up with two more clues that will help solve the mystery. Groups take turns reading their clues, as other groups take turns guessing the mystery person.

After each group has had a turn, point out that the seven clues did not help identify the mystery person. But, all could apply to Mrs. Ashton who is being sexually harassed. Examine each of the first seven statements in terms of feelings and behaviors, giving attention to how they are related to being sexually harassed.

My Body

Ask group members to think about their own body. This is done privately, perhaps written down on a piece of paper: Is it attractive? What are the attractive parts of your body? The most unattractive parts? Where do you get your notions of what is attractive and what is unattractive? How do TV programs and commercials affect your ideas about attractive and unattractive people? How does your body influence the things that you like to do? How would others describe you—attractive or unattractive? Do attractive people get harassed more than those who are less attractive? On a scale of one to ten, with 1 as low and 10 has high, how would you rate the problems of those who are attractive? The problems of those who are unattractive?

I Want You To...

Sometimes it is important to make your wants and wishes known to people. It might even be a demand. You can begin with "What would make life better for you?" "If you could change something about somebody, what would that be?" What do you think your teacher might say if he or she said, "I want this class to...."

Each person is encouraged to write a list of 10 demands. They may begin with "I demand that you...." or "I want you to...." Start by naming the person, or a pseudonym, and then finishing the sentence. For instance, "Amy, I want you stop interrupting me when I am talking to you." Or, "Brian, I demand that you quit punching me on the shoulder, even if it's just in fun."

Ask the group how they felt about writing their demands. Can they identify the two that were the most difficult to make? How hard would it be to actually make these demands?

Finally, relate this experience to the value and the problem of someone being sexually harassed to take a stand against perpetrators. Why is it hard for victims to make demands? Does making a demand mean that it will honored? What if it is refused? How can a person state a demand so that there is a better chance of it being honored?

Russell A. Sabella, Ph.D. & Robert D. Myrick, Ph.D.

The Nightly News

Imagine that you are going to be featured on the nightly news of your local television station. The TV spot will show you doing things of which you are proud. What are two things that you have done in school or at home this week that you hope will be shown. Then, just before ending, the announcer says that next week they will feature how you relate and get along with others, especially of the opposite gender. They are going to interview others to discover the things that you say and do. What will you want to edit or change to keep your friends and parents from seeing? What do you want to do this week to improve your image? What are things that you might have said or done that might be viewed as sexual harassment?

Enclosure

A volunteer sits in the corner of a room, while other group members go to the remaining corners. Then, everyone walks slowly and menacingly toward the volunteer who must stay in his or her corner. The convergence continues until the volunteer begins to cite a favorite childhood rhyme or sing a song. When this happens everyone must stop (freeze) and stare. The volunteer is then free to flee.

The volunteers in this situation often feel pressured, trapped and even crushed. After three or four volunteers have taken a turn, discuss the activity. What did the participants experience? How is the experience related to a person who feels that he or she being crushed or cornered through harassment.

Complete the Sentences

Group members complete the following incomplete sentences. This may be done in written form or aloud in a go-around.

- Boys pester and harass girls because....
- When sexually harassed, girls will usually....
- When I am embarrassed, I....
- When I get angry, I....
- When I feel put-down by someone, I....
- When someone is being sexually harassed he or she should....
- The worst thing about sexual harassment is....
- Someone who sexually harasses another person is probably feeling....
- Someone who is being sexually harassed is probably feeling....

Participants talk about the activity, telling which one was the hardest to complete. Which one was easiest?

Russell A. Sabella, Ph.D. & Robert D. Myrick, Ph.D.

Red Light, Green Light, Yellow Light

Three colored cards (red, yellow, green) are used in a game to help participants understand how people give signals about relationships. Discuss how traffic lights are similar to signals that people use in personal relationships. How can a person tell if he or she has a "green light" and should continue to flirt or make advances? What kinds of actions indicate that a person is wary and uncertain? What signals indicate that a person wants the other person to stop and make no further advances?

Using the following words, and others that might apply, discuss how "running a red light" is against the law and can lead to undesirable consequences. How is this similar to flirting that is welcomed and that which is not? At what point is a person entering a sexual harassment area? What should a person do when they receive a "yellow light" from someone who they would like to date?

The following list of feeling words and their relationship to one of the colored lights might put on a transparency and projected on a screen. It could help the participants determine the color light that they are receiving.

Green	Yellow	Red
courteous	awkward	discourteous
careful	cautious	aggressive
charming	intrigued	pushy
engaging	uncertain	loathsome
complimentary	mixed	confronting
valued	unsure	disliked
reciprocal	hesitant	resisted
flattered	perplexed	offended
shared	give & take	one-way
bold	bashful	aggressive
responsive	indefinite	unyielding
safe	risky	dangerous
attracted	inclined	repelled

Encourage the participants to think of other words and phrases that reflect feelings and related behaviors in terms of green, yellow, and red lights as interpersonal signals.

Is it possible to win someone over, if the person is initially resistant or uncertain? How? What happens to people who don't understand or respond to traffic lights? What about interpersonal signals? How is this related to sexual harassment?

Debate

Divide the group into about four debate teams. Two teams are brought to the front of the room and, by a chance drawing, one team argues "True" and the other "Not True" to debate questions such as those below. Teams are given five minutes to make a list of arguments to support their position to the question that they are debating. Then, the teams alternate in telling the audience (the other teams who are waiting their turn to debate) an argument or opinion to support their side of the debate. After all arguments have been heard, a few minutes is given to a discussion. The audience might ask questions of the teams. A vote of the audience might be taken to determine which team was winning at the point when time was called. Next, other teams debate another question.

- A person who cheats in one situation is likely to cheat in other situations.

- If you hear a person gossip or put someone down, this person is probably going to gossip or put you down someday.

- Sexual harassment leads to sexual violence.

- Only boys should do the asking, when it comes to dating.

- Saying "No" doesn't necessarily mean "No."

A Boy Who... (Rank Order)

Place the following items on a transparency to be shown on a screen or on pieces of paper to be distributed to a group. Participants first rate each of the items in terms of a five point continuum (1: Very Serious Problem to 5: Not A Serious Problem.) After the ratings, small groups are formed in which each group ranks the top three problems that are the most serious problems.

A boy who:

1. Cheats on a test.
2. Brags about himself.
3. Says ugly things about a teacher.
4. Fails a test, then lies about "not studying for it."
5. Makes sexual comments about girls to friends.
6. Teases a girl by making fun of her breasts.
7. Won't let a girl pass in the hallway without making a sexual remark.
8. Doesn't clean his fingernails.
9. Wears hand-me-down clothes.
10. Swears or uses profane language.
11. Smokes cigarettes.
12. Skips school to watch TV at home.
13. Forges his parents signature on an excused absence.
14. Says that he lost his homework assignment when in fact he never did it.
15. Says he has kissed a girl, when he hasn't.
16. Will cheat in order to win.
17. Blames others for his problems.
18. Lied to the principal to protect his best friend who was accused of lying to the principal.
19. Heard sexual harassing comments but denied that he heard them when asked by the principal.
20. Thinks it OK to sexually harass girls.
21. Uses clothes to get attention.
22. Tells a joke about sex.

Order in the Court

Participants are divided into small groups. Each group writes four skits or scenarios that focus on sexual harassment. For example:

1. A new student tries to impress a group of boys by teasing some girls.

2. A girl begins teasing a boy, who in turn, gets mad and retaliates with some negative comments.

3. Two boys pass a note which has crude types of pornographic drawings. A girl grabs the note and says she is going to read it to the shock of the boys.

4. A boy and his girlfriend have broken their close relationship and are dating others. They talk negatively about each other, including some exaggerations.

Cases are presented before the others, who act as an audience. From the audience a panel of three judges vote to decide 1) whether someone is guilty of sexual harassment; and, 2) some appropriate consequences. The panel's decisions are then compared to the audience's vote and are open for discussion.

Masks

Paper masks might be created to portray male and female faces. Girls and boys can then practice role reversals, using the masks in skits or perhaps reading a prepared dialogue.

The masks might also be used to illustrate the basic personality features associated with sexual harassment. A skit featuring the masks as alter-egos, following characters in the play to show emotions or motives, might be developed.

Is there a difference between thinking about doing something and actually doing it? Is there a difference between thinking repulsive things about people and saying repulsive things to them? Is tolerating something and doing nothing about it the same as supporting it?

Create skits or role-playing situations that illustrate people doing things. There is a moderator, who on occasion calls "Stop Action." Those who are holding alter-ego masks and following along side of the characters in the skit, are then asked to voice what the character might be thinking. Discuss the difference between thinking something and doing something in terms of social consequences, for better and for worse.

To Build a House of Cards

A deck of playing cards is given to an individual. He or she is to build a house of cards, leaning the cards next to and on top of others. A game is played by keeping score of the number of cards that were used before the house of cards fell down.

The activity might begin with a demonstration. A volunteer is asked to build a house of cards while others watch. A score is determined. A second try is then given; however, this time the builder is harassed by two or three other individuals while doing the task. The harassers cannot touch the builder, but they may do things that attempt to distract the builder.

If several decks of cards are available, the large group might be divided into smaller groups in order for everyone to have a chance to be a builder with and without harassment from others. This also gives everyone a chance to play the role of harasser and victim.

A large group discussion begins by asking how participants felt about the activity. What did some of the builders do in order to resist the harassment that they received? What behaviors and apparent feelings did participants notice among the harassers who were trying to distract the builders? What did successful builders do in order to continue with the task? Look for and talk about other feelings and actions that the game or activity elicited and that might be related to issues of being a harasser, as well as a victim.

The Mannequins

A person is selected to be a Spotter. Five to seven other participants are asked to be Mannequins. As a group they stand before the remaining participants in order to play the game. The Spotter is in the middle of a circle of Mannequins, who on the count of 1, 2, 3, freeze themselves and make no movements. The Spotter looks around the circle and tries to discover anyone who is moving their heads, arms, legs, fingers, or eyes. When the Spotter sees movement from a person, then he or she is eliminated.

This might also be done by bringing three participants in front of the class, with one Spotter. The task is to remain motionless. The last one eliminated in each triad is the winner. Then, winners of the triads are matched against each other until there is a final winner.

A discussion focuses on how hard it was to see people doing things, as well as how difficult it was to be motionless. This can lead to more discussion about how difficult it is for people to control or restrict themselves. What kind of society would we have if everyone were confined to moving like a mannequin, for fear of offending someone? Are guidelines for sexual harassment too restricting? Do they make people feel like mannequins around others? Or, do they enable people to be more spontaneous and free to move?

Listen to the Music

Encourage group participants to bring in some popular songs and music. As a group, analyze the lyrics. What is the message of the lyrics? Are there any put-downs? What makes sexually harassing language popular among song writers and listeners? What makes some musical performers want to create an image of being rebels and harassers?. How does this appeal to people?

What's Happening Here?

Participants look at slide pictures that are projected on a screen or pictures that are passed around the group. The slides or pictures show adolescents in situations that may or may not constitute sexual harassment. (e.g., a female walking down the hall, with a group of boys looking at her and one boy appearing to yell something).

After a picture is shown, the group is asked, "What is happening in this picture?" "How can you tell" "What do you think took place just before this picture was taken?" "What is going to happen next?"

Talk about how the pictures tended to create several different stories. Some were positive and others were negative. Was it the picture or events surrounding the picture that made the difference? Do people have different perceptions of an event? How is this related to sexual harassment?

The Feedback Chair

An empty chair is placed in front of a group of five participants. The group is asked to imagine that someone they like and enjoy being around is sitting in the chair. They take turns giving the person a compliment, using the following three steps:

1. "One of the things I have noticed about you is...." (Be specific and give an example)

2. "This makes me feel...." (A pleasant feeling word).

3. "And this makes me want to.... (Say or do something).

After compliments are practiced, another go-around with the empty chair can feature a confrontation. The same three steps are followed, but in the second part the emphasis is on an unpleasant feeling.

Discuss how what a person does might bring about a pleasant or an unpleasant feeling. Certain behaviors do not always elicit the same feelings, as it depends upon the person who is there when the action takes place. How could this feedback model be used to communicate to a harasser? Could the steps be written down in a letter? If someone is being treated with respect, should that person take time and give a compliment? Or, is it best to wait until you have an unpleasant feeling and then confront a person?

Mobile

A group (family, classroom, school, etc.) can be seen as a mobile. Hang a mobile from the ceiling. In this case, different shaped figures of different sizes are strung together and balanced. When one is pulled, all of them move or jiggle. When each part is stilled, the entire mobile is still.

Discuss how close-knit groups develop invisible connectors between people who live or work together. Actions by one person can affect the actions of others, such as when one part of a mobile is touched. There is a ripple effect.

Can the mobile be used to help describe the environment of a school? A family? A community?

How is sexual harassment of someone in school able to affect the learning environment, even if others were not there at the time it happened?

Crossword Puzzle

Often times, students enjoy the challenge of a crossword puzzle. This puzzle contains clues to words that involve knowledge, attitudes, and behaviors about sexual harassment. The answers are provided in the form of a word list and a puzzle key. Students can work on this individually, in pairs, or in groups. Some facilitators have had pairs of students compete for who can complete the puzzle the quickest, having all the correct answers, of course.

ADULT	HELP
ATTENDANCE	HOSTILE
ATTITUDE	HURT
AVOID	ILLEGAL
AWARENESS	JOURNAL
BEHAVIOR	KNOWLEDGE
BLAME	LAW
BLIND	LIABILITY
BOYS	LISTENING
COMMUNICATION	MEAN
CONFIDENCE	MUTUAL
CONSENT	MYTH
CONTROL	PARENT
EDUCATION	PERFORMANCE
EIGHTY	PERPETRATOR
ENVIRONMENT	PHYSICAL
FACT	RELATIONSHIP
FEAR	REPORT
FEELINGS	SCHOOL
GIRLS	SEXUAL
GRADES	SUIT
HALLWAY	VICTIM
HARASSMENT	VISUAL

Crossword Puzzle

Across

1. Responsibility
4. An older person who may help
7. Helps reduce the risk
10. One place to get your education
11. Half of the solution
13. Half of the solution
14. Sexual harassment reduces this
20. Person guilty of sexual harassment
21. Keep one of these for reporting
23. Where it happens most often
24. Breaking it can land you in jail
25. Older person who can help
26. Having a great deal of influence
27. Scared
30. Type of illegal harassment
32. You might need this if hurt
33. The target of sexual harassment
34. Place that can be hostile
35. What you know
37. Measure of success
39. Aggressive; mean
41. Can be positive or negative
42. Sexual harassment reduces this
44. A form of sexual harassment
45. Sexual harassment you can see
46. Believing In yourself

Down

2. Your actions
3. Good discussion
5. Are you here today?
6. Percent of kids sexually harassed
8. Can cost you money
9. Give permission
11. Against the law
15. A belief that is not true
16. Can be sexual
17. Depending on two people
18. Do this with words and feelings
19. How you grow together
22. Never do this to the victim
27. Not fiction
28. When you cannot see
29. To not participate
31. Emotions
36. The more you have, the more you want
38. Can be positive or negative
39. Opposite of help
40. You write one of these
43. A reason why people harass

Russell A. Sabella, Ph.D. & Robert D. Myrick, Ph.D.

Crossword Puzzle

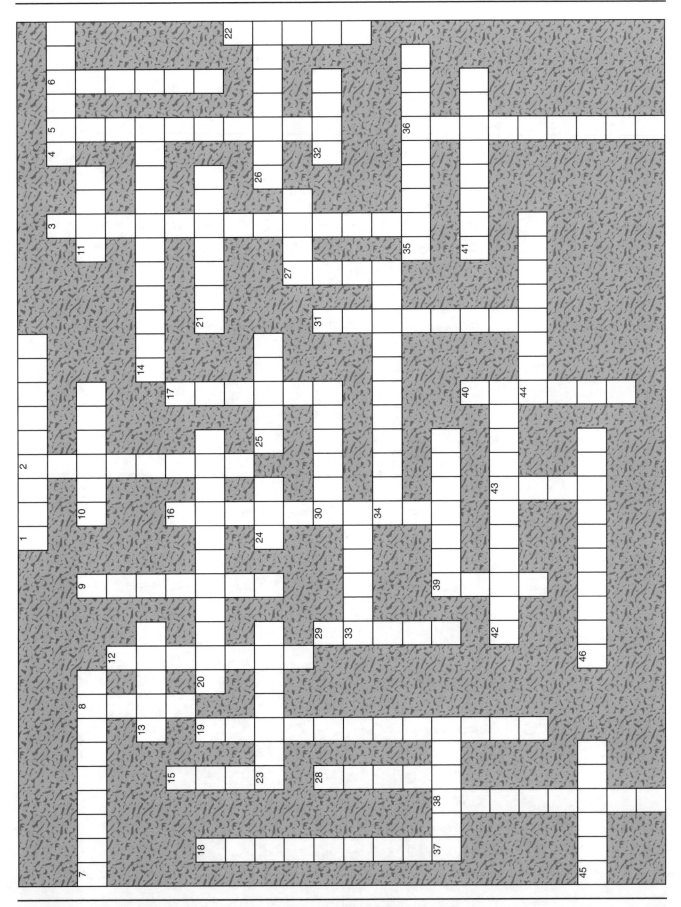

Crossword Puzzle Answers

Russell A. Sabella, Ph.D. & Robert D. Myrick, Ph.D.

The Facilitative Model and Group Leadership

Well-designed guidance units are not successful by themselves. They require group leaders who are knowledgeable about the topic, have a positive attitude towards students, and can effectively manage and facilitate a group. This chapter describes some skills for facilitating group activities such as those about sexual harassment. The skills, when used systematically and combined for effect, have been referred to as the Facilitative Model (Myrick, 1993).

A facilitator is someone who is adept in the use of interpersonal skills and who can assist individuals or groups to move toward their goals. In this case, the goals include knowledge, attitudes, and behaviors which contribute to positive and mutually respectful relationships. Facilitators help students explore their ideas, examine their behaviors, and make responsible decisions. They look for innovative, effective, and relatively simple techniques to give them direction when they are working with others.

The Facilitative Model consists of a few basic interpersonal concepts and related skills.

The Facilitative Model consists of a few basic interpersonal concepts and related skills. Although similar ones have evolved over the years, this model is a unique package of selected concepts and skills that are systematically organized and linked together. It consists of four parts: 1) facilitative conditions, which influence helping relationships; 2) facilitative processes, which give a focus to the interaction that takes place; 3) facilitative responses, which suggest ways in which to lead and respond to participants; and 4) facilitative activities and tasks, which help expedite learning. Let us take a look at how these can be applied to facilitating a group unit about harassment.

The Facilitative Conditions

Confronting sexual harassment involves teaching facts and studying actions that are often confusing, misunderstood, and loaded with emotions. To have a healthy and productive discussion of the issues, participants are obliged to treat others with respect and understanding. Although it can be difficult to be open to new ideas and listen to others as they talk about sensitive issues, that is part of the process of improving personal and working relationships. It is the goal of all group facilitators to help create interpersonal conditions that enable members to speak freely and to have serious, as well as lighthearted, discussions.

There appears to be six core conditions....

Scholars may propose several different conditions that affect interpersonal relationships and, subsequently, open group discussions (e.g., genuineness, interest, specificity, and a willingness to listen to others). For our purposes, there appears to be six core conditions that need to be given careful consideration: *respect, understanding, caring, acceptance, friendliness,* and *trustworthiness*. While others might be added, let's take a closer look at these six.

Respect suggests that common courtesies are extended to people, including the right to express one's own ideas and feelings, and to be responsible for personal decisions and actions. In the area of sexual harassment, you may hear a student say, "Girls who dress in sexy ways deserve to be harassed. They get what's coming to them." Considering the laws of the land, this belief dismisses the right of persons to dress as they choose. It is a judgmental statement that blames the victim. It suggests that the eye of the beholder is more important than the rights of an individual.

A group leader might worry about a student who holds this idea to be true and feel compelled to immediately confront and change that belief to one that is more respectful and compassionate. People who disrespect the rights of others still need respect themselves if they are to explore all points of view and study the implications of their statements. It is important that the facilitator model this condition and encourage others to do the same. Later we will consider how this might be done.

Understanding is frequently used to express the idea that a person has grasped the meaning of a concept or term. At times, it suggests that a person has a knowledge base and is able to comprehend the facts of a matter. It is also used to describe the phenomenon of perceiving and acknowledging what another person is experiencing. There is empathy, which is the communication that one is aware of what a person is feeling. Understanding, in this case, goes beyond a knowledge of events in a person's life and touches the emotional experiences. It is particularly needed in the area of intergender communication—a vital part of preventing sexual harassment.

Men and women generally embrace different perspectives when they communicate. Their respective styles and approaches can differ and sometimes clash. For instance, Tannen (1990) wrote that gender differences exist and that recognizing them can free individuals to be more open to one another. Differences can be taken into account, adjustments can be made, and communication styles can be respected. In terms of understanding others, she said:

> *Much—even most—meaning in conversation does not reside in the words spoken at all, but is filled-in by the person listening. Each of us decides whether we think others are speaking in the spirit of differing status or symmetrical connection. The likelihood that individuals will tend to interpret someone else's words as one or the other depends more on the hearer's own focus, concerns, and habits than on the spirit in which the words were intended (p. 37).*

Understanding what another person is experiencing means going beyond the words that are used to describe an event or episode in one's life. Careful attention is given to how the person is talking, the words that are chosen, and what the person might be sensing. When this condition is present between individuals or within a group, the foundation is laid for further in-depth awareness and knowledge.

Caring suggests that you are personally interested and concerned about a person's well-being. It involves a sense of personal commitment to the person because you give something of yourself in the relationship. You value the person enough to psychologically reach out and be attentive. When a group leader genuinely cares for people and models this for students, chances are good the students will then care for one another. This contributes to a learning environment which is safe and nurturing.

An effective group discussion of harassment is grounded in the sense that people care about each other.

An effective group discussion of harassment is grounded in the sense that people care about each other. A student who nonchalantly makes crude remarks or makes inappropriate jests at the expense of others shows both a lack of respect and caring. When someone says, "I don't care," it is a devastating blow to a relationship. It dismisses the person's being. Without caring there is no sympathy, no tenderness, no compassion, no willingness to be involved. The lack of caring indicates an indifference or apathy that may well be at the center of tolerating harassment and harm to others.

A group facilitator knows that caring is also a motivating force to learn more about others and to consider their interests and rights. Many adolescents appear to be so self-centered that their actions imply that they don't care about others. In fact, the opinions of others during this stage of life generally matters a great deal to them. A discussion about harassment and its consequences can be appealing to young people who want the favorable attention of their peers. As knowledge, respect, and understanding increase, so does caring.

Acceptance is a willingness to believe in and acknowledge the worth and dignity of a person, despite the circumstances. We can be accepting of someone and still not agree with the person's ideas and/or behaviors. One's behavior can be challenged or ignored, if necessary, but the value of the person as a human being is always present.

It is difficult, at times, to imagine how you could accept a person who has done something which hurts others. This becomes even more difficult when the acts are despicable and offensive. The mistake is to focus only on the unacceptable behavior. For instance, suppose you hear a young man say something that is clearly a put-down of a girl who happens to be standing nearby. You may choose to confront the boy about his language which is unacceptable to you, but your demeanor might be more effective if you view him as a worthwhile person who has simply behaved inappropriately.

The condition of acceptance should be modeled and needs to be addressed from the beginning. Only when students feel that they will continue to be an important part of the group, even in the face of unpopular responses, will they fully participate in the activities. As the saying goes, "There are no stupid questions."

Friendliness communicates a warm personal style that invites others to reciprocate mutual interest and warmth. It is a factor which often results from the presence of the other facilitative conditions. But, in its own right, friendliness is best characterized as a kindly attitude in which there are amiable exchanges and a genuine sense of comfort and support. It is characterized by an ease of being together.

Friendly chats about difficult topics may seem hard to imagine. After all, sexual harassment is a somber subject that needs to be given serious consideration. Yet, students are more likely to talk about the topic when they are in friendly territory and do not have to worry about defending themselves. When a group is congenial and supportive, there is a greater likelihood the members will participate in the activities, cooperate on the tasks, and enjoy learning together.

Trustworthiness is being entrusted with confidence or a sense of security. It often inspires faith and reliance, but it is primarily founded on a prediction that someone will act in an honest and forthright manner so an individual's well-being is not hurt. How much, and to which level, students offer information or take part in activities depends on how much they trust the facilitator and others in their group. Students want to know what they share will not become the subject of gossip and repeated outside the group. They want to trust their comments will not be taken out of context and met with ridicule. Sometimes, no matter how much effort a leader puts into creating the condition of trustworthiness, students will not make comments or ask questions because they do not trust the members of the group. Most of the time, however, a few warm-up activities where group members learn more about each other and a frank discussion of group ground rules can make a positive difference.

...students are more likely to talk about the topic when they are in friendly territory and do not have to worry about defending themselves.

The Facilitative Processes

"Okay," you may be thinking, "but if I'm friendly and have a good working relationship with students, then what happens?" The answer to that question depends on what you want to help happen in the group. What group dynamics do you want to encourage? What is the group process you hope to mobilize? What are the group processes that will help students gain the most from activities and discussions?

The facilitative processes refer to group interactions and interpersonal relationships.

The facilitative processes refer to group interactions and interpersonal relationships. Each of four processes has its own special attribute and emerges because of the reciprocal reactions of facilitator and group members. The group processes are also interactive, with one influencing another. They are unique products of the communication of ideas, feelings, and behaviors in a helping relationship.

Although others may cite more considerations, there are four desired group processes that are part of the Facilitative Model: 1) self-disclosure; 2) feedback; 3) increased awareness and decision making; and 4) responsible action (Myrick, 1993).

Student Self-Disclosure

Self-disclosure involves revealing one's self to others. As the trust relationship builds among group members, whether in an academic class or a group counseling session, there is more sharing of personal information and greater depth in exploring private ideas and feelings, no matter what the topic.

We have all had experiences in our lives which made a significant impact on us. Sometimes we remember the events vividly and at other times we can only recall the general effect they had on us, but strong feelings and impressions linger. The events may not be nearly as important as the meaning we gave them at the time. Self-disclosure involves revealing feelings, life events, ideas, and opinions. It is an expression of self.

Talking about feelings and ideas can be useful as we examine the nature of sexual harassment and it's impact on society. Even though they may not have experienced it, many students will still have their own reactions to hearing about it, to studying it, and to thinking of what they might do in certain situations. They have opinions about what might or might not be done. Some students may choose to tell about a time when they were harassed or when they saw someone else being victimized.

Self-disclosure can have a strong cathartic value for students.

Self-disclosure can have a strong cathartic value for students. There may be times when students need to blurt out their feelings just to drain away some tension. They might talk rapidly and impulsively in an attempt to "get it off their chest"—to hear how their ideas sound to themselves as much as to others. One way of helping students sort out their ideas and feelings is to encourage them to disclose more and to explore their ideas with them. Such a process can help them to gain a better picture of themselves and how the issue of sexual harassment affects them.

Students have many opportunities to talk about ideas related to their academic classes, but here are fewer opportunities to talk about their social relationships, including the interpersonal events that take place at school. Even when they talk with others casually about what is on their minds, they seldom are in situations where they can share their feelings and ideas in depth. They rarely have chances to discuss a topic to any great length because somebody is usually changing the topic or taking the focus away from them.

The facilitative conditions of respect, understanding, caring, acceptance, friendliness, and trustworthiness will foster and support student self-disclosure. Many students guard what they say at school and need time to adjust to a more facilitative environment. Such students may see school as an environment where they receive subtle, and sometimes blatant, messages that warn them to be careful and cautious about what they say. Sometimes students do not "open up" to say what is really on their minds for fear they will be met with critical evaluations or put-downs.

It is very difficult to help students assess themselves or to change their ideas, attitudes, and behaviors if you do not know what they are thinking or feeling. Therefore, when providing the unit about sexual harassment, you will want to create situations and an atmosphere in which students can self-disclose and talk openly about matters.

Facilitator Self-Disclosure

On occasion counselors and teachers are told they should not reveal their own personal ideas, feelings, and values to students. It is assumed that students will be unduly influenced by such ideas, feelings, values, and decisions. In a sense, everything you do while you are with others reveals something about yourself. Your choice of words, for example, may tell how you feel and what you value. Or they may reveal your attitude or a hidden agenda you are carrying to a session or activity. You cannot avoid divulging some things about yourself when facilitating a group, even if you try. But, what and how much should you self-disclose?

Most students have heard parents and teachers tell about their student days, "the good old days." "When I was a kid, I had to..." is an opening line that is a sure bet to turn students away. For the most part, students have a tough time imagining adults—especially teachers and counselors—as young people their age.

Most adults usually go too far when they self-disclose things about themselves. They tell too many details and they do not share enough of their feelings. They seldom miss having a moral to the story. The bottom line is usually, "So, I understand what you are going through, and therefore...." It may even have the ring of, "That's what happened to me, here's what I did, and this is what you can do (or should not do)." Students frequently hear advice more than a genuine shared experience.

...everything you do while you are with others reveals something about yourself.

Russell A. Sabella, Ph.D. & Robert D. Myrick, Ph.D.

To avoid falling into old cliches and boring students with stories about days past, try to disclose more of your feelings rather than the details of a personal situation. Be cautious when telling students how you solved a similar problem or how you turned a potential disaster into a smashing success. Rather, emphasize what you were feeling during those times.

For example, consider the following self-disclosure by a facilitator who had a female student talk about a time when someone was staring at her:

I remember once when someone wouldn't stop looking me up and down as I passed by. I was embarrassed at first and then I got angry. I also remember being afraid since I didn't know much about this person and wasn't sure about what really was going on.

Notice how the facilitator, in this case, communicated what was thought to be a similar experience. In contrast, the following would probably be less effective:

I remember once when someone kept looking at me, staring at me. I knew what he was thinking. All I had on was a jumper. No big deal. I suddenly turned and yelled at him in front of the others that were there too. "What you see is what you don't get, Stupid!" You should have seen the expression on his face. All his friends standing there laughed at him. He deserved to be put-down for what he was doing. That's what you need to do, just speak up and embarrass him back.

Although interesting, this disclosure runs the risk of being only tangential to what the student is experiencing. Most attention is directed to the events of the time and the assumption is these events add credibility to the advice that is to follow.

If you focus primarily on the feelings you experienced in a situation and less on the event itself, then you are likely to build a bond that cuts across differences. This is particularly true as you work with students of a different race, sex, economic, or cultural background. Similar feelings bridge communication gaps more than similar events or situations. Self-disclosure will be a mutual experience for you and your students as you work with them. The appropriateness, timeliness, and the extent of personal disclosure will result from your professional judgment and skill.

The self-disclosure process sets the foundation for other facilitative processes. As students disclose more about themselves in the activities, they can receive feedback from others about their ideas, feelings, attitudes, and behaviors. The two facilitative processes of self-disclosure and feedback interact together to create a free and open relationship as the facilitative conditions continue to grow. It is then that students explore their ideas in greater depth, evaluate their feelings more honestly, examine alternatives, make responsible decisions, and find solutions to problems.

If you focus primarily on the feelings you experienced in a situation and less on the event itself, then you are likely to build a bond that cuts across differences.

Feedback

Feedback is a term that probably had its origin in electronics and engineering. It implies that a circuit is looped back to its original source and this flow back allows for a modification of an effect that produced the results.

Feedback from others can help us stay on track or chart a new direction.

For example, the thermostats in your home use information about temperature to activate air conditioning or heating units. Commercial airline pilots use guidance systems that involve feeding information into computers and then confirming or correcting the airplane's flight pattern.

In a similar sense, personal feedback is helpful to us as individuals. It sometime validates our attitudes and behaviors. At other times, it helps us modify or make changes in our lives. Feedback from others can help us stay on track or chart a new direction. There are several possible sources of data that can be used in feedback, including tests and inventories. But, personal information and reaction from peers is most valuable.

Increased Awareness and Decision Making

The third facilitative process which a group facilitator tries to foster is that of increased awareness and decision making. It is assumed that as a consequence of self-disclosure and receiving feedback, a person is more aware of his or her impact on others, as well as ideas and concepts. The first two processes create a climate in which information can be received, concepts can be explored, insights can be gained, goals and objectives can be identified, and decisions can be made. It is this process that most people want to experience when they are trying to resolve a problem or issue.

Most students who take part in a guidance unit about sexual harassment want to know more about the problem as it affects their lives. They tend to personalize information and apply it to themselves. If it has meaning, then they listen and make decisions. If it has no meaning, then there is no special awareness and no attempt to resolve a problem.

One student knew that she didn't like what some boys kept saying to her. She learned that it was sexual harassment and this awareness led her to consider some actions she might take. She discussed her situation with classmates, carefully considering alternatives, as she tried to sort out what she might do. Eventually, she decided it was time to be more assertive and tell the boys how their behaviors made her feel and what she intended to do about it if they continued.

Once a problem has been identified and clarified, it is time to consider what might take place next. This is not the same as taking action, but it is the preceding step. A person may think through a problem, considering all the events, feelings, and possibilities. But the thinking process may not produce any results until it is acted upon.

Responsible Action

Responsible action is the final process. In this case, decisions have been made, alternatives have been considered, and a plan of action has been mapped. The next step focuses on the person(s) involved to do something about the problem or situation.

The ultimate goal for *Confronting Sexual Harassment* includes enhancing knowledge, behaviors, and attitudes conducive to mutually respectful and healthy relationships. This is incompatible with sexual harassment which is one-sided and destructive. With increased awareness of sexual harassment issues and how one feels about them comes the ability to consider alternative courses of action. As students think about what they can do and the consequences of any action they might take, they gain a clearer picture of their own rights and responsibilities. Eventually, they are encouraged to take a stand against inappropriate social behavior and to help prevent sexual harassment. But, it must be done in a responsible manner.

The guidance unit about sexual harassment is designed to allow students to be responsible for taking action.

The guidance unit about sexual harassment is designed to allow students to be responsible for taking action. Facilitators need to resist the urge to rush in and act for the student. For example, rather than quickly telling students about what they should and should not do, timely information and learning activities allows them to deduce the critical issues and inspires responsibility.

The facilitative processes during the guidance unit are directly related to what students do and say in the time they are together. Therefore, special attention needs to be given to how people talk with one another as they attempt to develop facilitative conditions and processes.

Certain verbal responses—called high facilitative responses—and congenial nonverbal behaviors increase the probability that a group leader or facilitator will be seen as friendly, caring, understanding, accepting, and trustworthy. This, in turn, sets the stage for self-disclosure and an open exploration of issues related to harassment. It opens the door for personal feedback, where students can tell one another how certain behaviors affect them. As facilitative responses increase in frequency and relevant information is introduced, the stage is set for increased awareness and decision making. Self-confidence results and leads to responsible action.

The High Facilitative Responses

There are six basic responses that are the foundation of the Facilitative Model. You will want to increase the frequency of them in your work. They are 1) the feeling-focused response; 2) the clarifying or summarizing response; 3) the open question; 4) facilitative feedback, as a compliment or confrontation; 5) simple acknowledgment; and 6) linking (Myrick, 1993).

The Feeling-Focused Response

The feeling-focused response is one of the three highest facilitative responses you can make to others. It is an attempt to surpass the events or ideas being expressed and to capture the essence of a person's experience. It directs attention to what a person is feeling.

Some writers have referred to this type of response as "reflecting empathy," knowing that people feel better understood when someone senses what they are feeling in a situation and mirrors back their feelings. For instance, you probably feel most understood when someone has somehow communicated he or she has the essence of what you are experiencing. It is more than the words that describe your ideas or the events you are experiencing.

...people feel better understood when someone senses what they are feeling in a situation....

Here are some examples of feeling-focused responses:

"You're really angry, John."

"Jennifer, you seemed confused."

"That was exciting for you."

"You had fun during that activity."

"It makes you disappointed to hear about it."

"You're feeling more confident now."

The words citing feelings are the key ingredients in these empathic statements. A feeling word has to be present in this type of response. It cannot be assumed you understand and know what the person is experiencing. You have to say or do something to show it.

You have probably heard the old adage, "Put yourself in the other person's shoes." It suggests that by doing so you will be more understanding. You could also ask yourself, "How would I feel if I were to say something like that?" Or, "How would I have to feel to do something like that?"

The answer to these questions might give you some insight as to what the person is experiencing. They might lead you to be more empathic. However, the problem with this approach is it sometimes traps you into projecting your own feelings on others. We often assume others experience things the same way we do, whereas this may not be true. For instance, if you have seen or experienced sexual harassment, you must guard against projecting your own experiences and feelings on others. Even though the event may seem similar, the characters are different. It occurred at a different time and there were likely to have been some unique experiences. Listen for them and let the person know that you understand through a focus on the feelings, rather than on what you once experienced.

It is not enough to identify the feelings and say nothing.

Being perceived as an empathic listener—one who responds accurately to what a person is experiencing—requires you to tune into the person's feelings and then respond. It is not enough to identify the feelings and say nothing. It is never enough to say simply, "I understand what you went through" or "I know how you feel." Neither of these statements communicate understanding.

Pleasant and unpleasant feelings. One helpful method that can make you a more empathic person is to listen for the feelings that go beyond the literal sense of the words. Ask yourself, "Am I hearing pleasant feelings, unpleasant feelings, or both?" This will give you some clues regarding what the person is experiencing. A list of pleasant and unpleasant feeling words is presented in Figure 7.1. Review the list. Which words are most familiar to you? Which ones are most related to when a person is having a problem? Which ones are likely to present themselves in the *Confronting Sexual Harassment* unit? Which ones are unfamiliar to you or sound strange? What are some current slang expressions which students use to tell about their feelings which could be added to the list?

Figure 7.1

Feeling Words

Pleasant		Unpleasant	
accepted	needed	abused	guarded
appreciated	optimistic	angry	hateful
bright	peaceful	annoyed	irritated
calm	pleased	bored	offended
cheerful	powerful	concerned	overwhelmed
close	proud	confused	pained
confident	refreshed	cramped	pressured
contented	relaxed	defeated	rejected
delighted	relieved	defensive	sad
enjoyment	satisfied	depressed	sore
excited	secure	disappointed	suspicious
happy	special	discouraged	threatened
hopeful	stimulated	disgusted	tired
important	strong	doubtful	troubled
inspired	successful	empty	uncomfortable
interested	trusting	fearful	uneasy
joyful	uplifted	fragmented	unhappy
loved	warm	gloomy	worried

Feeling-focused responses will help you be perceived as someone who cares, who is interested, and who is an attentive listener. Students will feel more comfortable and relaxed with you when you try to understand how they see things.

To begin a sentence with, "You feel...," does not necessarily mean that you will focus on a person's feelings. For instance, "You feel that sexual harassment is a problem." This statement is not a feeling-focused response. It is really directed to the student's opinion or idea. It might be stated, "You're concerned that it could be a big problem in our school."

The first part focuses on the feeling and the second part emphasizes the person's related thoughts.

Another response that is not feeling-focused is, "I feel that you should learn more about sexual harassment." This is an opinion. It suggests what the person should do. The response is not person-centered; it is a form of advice coming from someone else's experience.

To begin a sentence with, "You feel...," does not necessarily mean that you will focus on a person's feelings.

Russell A. Sabella, Ph.D. & Robert D. Myrick, Ph.D.

Nonverbal behavior and communication. Nonverbal communication is a part of the interaction that happens between people. It comes through in the tone of one's voice, the speed at which one speaks, the poignant pauses, and the slight hesitations that happen as a story is told. It includes stammering, stuttering, shouting, whispering, and other vocal expressions. It also entails facial expressions, hand gestures, foot movements, and body position.

Body messages are part of the communication process. Often the position or the movement of one's body will communicate whether one is experiencing pleasant or unpleasant feelings. A turn of the lip, a frown, a grinding of teeth, or a rolling of the eyes can be valuable clues as to what someone is thinking and feeling. Although an awareness of nonverbal behavior can be helpful in counseling and teaching, there is no reliable reference book which helps us analyze and interpret this type of behavior.

The Clarifying or Summarizing Response

If you are like most listeners, when a person is talking you will attend to the events or the ideas being talked about. They are the basis of the conversation and provide the framework for accurate understanding. Although emotion is part of expressing ideas, the thoughts and the story being communicated must also be understood.

After listening attentively, you may want to clarify a significant idea or summarize some themes that you heard expressed. For instance,

"You have already thought about the problem of sexual harassment."

"Let's see then, you think that boys and girls can get along better by talking with each other more and by being honest, even about sensitive issues as this one."

"You and your girlfriend disagree about the effect of wolf calls at people who walk by."

Clarifying or summarizing responses focus on basic ideas or events.

Clarifying or summarizing responses focus on basic ideas or events. In a free-flowing conversation or discussion, many things are communicated. One statement might express a key idea, such as a description of a hostile environment. Sometimes the person who is talking will veer off course and begin talking about something else, maybe introducing some more thoughts, that may or may not be relevant to the first idea expressed. Being an attentive listener is not an easy job, especially when a person is rambling about many things.

It can be helpful to make a clarifying or summarizing response when you: a) are not sure if you are following the person's train of thought; b) are not sure if you heard something correctly; or c) want to draw attention or emphasize something that was said. Such responses focus on the content of the discussion or the events of the story. There is no attempt to use feeling words, although feelings may be heard when the ideas were expressed.

As you try to focus the conversation or highlight a few ideas, use fresh words when you clarify or summarize. This helps you avoid parroting. You can use some of the same words, but turn the basic phrases around, unless you deliberately want to repeat the phrasing for emphasis. Some people have referred to this type of statement as paraphrasing, which is a rewording of the meaning expressed in something written or spoken.

Some typical lead-in phrases are:

"If I hear you correctly...."

"You seem to be saying...."

"If I am following you, you are saying...."

"In other words, you are trying to...."

"Correct me if I am wrong, but...."

"What I hear from what you have said is...."

"It strikes me that you are primarily...."

"I have heard these key ideas, 1)...."

"Let me see if I understand, you have said...."

"What is emerging from all that you said is...."

"Let's see, you are thinking that...."

Such phrases alert students that you are trying to focus the discussion or conversation. They also provide a little "wiggle room" or a simple qualification of what you are planning to clarify or summarize. Moreover, they provide you a lead as you attempt to express your own thoughts.

Suppose a student in a session said, "You know we are always talking about people who sexually harass others as being boys. I'm tired of it. I know plenty of girls who are doing this stuff." You might respond to the student's feelings (e.g., "It frustrates you when others always use boys as examples of perpetrators.") You might clarify or summarize (e.g., "You've noticed that most people talk about harassers as if it were only boys.") In both cases, you follow the lead of the student, rather than give advice or reassuring remarks, and this facilitates more communication.

The Open Question

...open questions ask for more information and encourage responses....

Asking questions that provoke thought and insight are effective when trying to get students to learn knowledge, skills, and attitudes which reduce the risk of sexual harassment. Questions can be either open or closed. Closed questions only require simple "yes" or "no" responses. They are sometimes experienced as a "just give me the facts" approach. On the other hand, open questions ask for more information and encourage responses with explanations. Look at these examples:

"Do you like learning about sexual harassment?" (closed)

"What can you tell me about sexual harassment?" (open)

"Did you talk with your parents about our activities?" (closed)

"What have you told your parents about our activities?" (open)

The open question provides a broad base from which to respond. There is some leeway and how the person responds may provide valuable clues and information. The closed question is narrow and only interested in the basic fact. Closed questions also tend to be couched in terms of your perspective, whereas open questions elicit the students' points of view.

Note the examples below. Which do you find more inviting?

"Is this term confusing you?" (closed)

"You don't understand, do you?" (closed)

"What is it that is confusing you?" (open)

"Are you going to participate today?" (closed)

"What can be done so you will participate today?" (open)

"What are your thoughts about public displays of affection?" (open)

Open questions are more facilitative because they invite additional disclosure. They encourage students to express themselves more. Closed questions, however, also have their value, especially if you are trying to get some specific information or confirm some thoughts or facts about something (e.g., "Did you complete the sexual harassment inventory?") There will be times when you can speed up information gathering or a learning activity by using closed questions, if that is what you want to accomplish.

The most facilitative open questions tend to begin with "What" or "How" instead of "Why."

The most facilitative open questions tend to begin with "What" or "How" instead of "Why." The latter is risky since it tends to ask people to explain or justify themselves (e.g., "Why do you believe only girls can be sexually harassed?") The "why" question deserves special attention.

Most people do not know the reasons they do the things they do (or have certain thoughts or attitudes). Yet, they might be asked, "Why did you do that?" Many students respond to such a question with a quick, "I don't know." They look away or shrug their shoulders. They feel on the spot. Look at these questions:

"Why don't you participate more?"

"Why did you say such an ugly thing to him?"

"Why do you always ask what we're going to do even though I've already explained it?"

"Why do you generalize to all boys?"

"Why is it difficult for you to think about this problem?"

How would you feel if such questions were directed to you? What kinds of answers are possible? What kinds of impact do you think they might make on students?

We may never discover or understand all the reasons we do the things we do. A rational explanation of some things seems almost impossible. In addition, the "why" question has also come to mean something else besides a question. It is often an opinion. Look again at the previous examples. Behind each of the questions is advice: Participate more; Do not say that to him; Listen to directions more; Don't generalize; Pay attention.

We may never discover or understand all the reasons we do the things we do.

When students hear the "why" in a question, they also hear criticism. They frequently get defensive, even when it is a legitimate question of interest or concern. Therefore, facilitative group leaders limit their use of this open question, knowing that it is not as productive as turning it into a "what" or "how" question. For example:

"Why did you say that to her?"

becomes

"What made you want to say that to her?"

"Why don't you like to participate in the activity?"

becomes

"What would want to make you want to participate more?"

The what and how questions are more specific and they are easier to answer. The why questions, although they may produce some insightful thought and comments, are usually less productive because they tend to elicit rationalizations and defensive postures. Clearly, the wording of a question—the way in which it is phrased or posed— can make a difference in the response that is received. Tone of voice can also make a difference. A question is a response to someone and it communicates your values and interests.

The Low Facilitative Responses

While all responses, at one time or another, might be helpful, some are likely to be less facilitative than others. Three common responses that are generally considered to be least facilitative are: a) advising; b) analyzing; and c) reassuring. Let us see how these fit into the facilitative model.

Advising

Advising is a category that describes responses which tell people how to behave. It judges behavior. For instance:

"Instead of arguing, you should see his point of view."

"Don't talk so much; let others have a turn to speak."

"Just ignore them and they will quit harassing you."

"One of the best things you can do is to apologize."

"If you would only be open to what they're saying, then you wouldn't feel as defensive."

Advice is cheap and it is given by almost everyone. Students hear a lot of advice from their parents, teachers, and counselors. It is easy to recognize and follows such lead-ins as:

"You should...."

"If I were you, I would...."

"The best way is to...."

"If you don't..., then...."

"If you would only...."

"You need to...."

"The thing to do is...."

When advice is relevant and practical, it can be helpful and it might facilitate people toward their goals

When advice is relevant and practical, it can be helpful and it might facilitate people toward their goals. This is especially true when it is offered at an appropriate time and is in the form of a suggestion instead of a command. Students will look to you for some timely advice and you will want to advise them on occasion. For example, you might have a student who comes for advice on how to handle a possible sexual harassment situation. For example, "You need to keep a log of all the incidents, with the time, date, and details describing what is happening to you." While this does shift the responsibility for decision making to you, it may be timely and worth the risk.

Advising and evaluating are rated as the least facilitative of responses for building helping or working relationships. Yet, they do have their place. It is the timely use of them that will make the critical difference.

Analyzing

Analyzing responses probably gained their popularity from the theory there is always a logical reason people do the things they do. And, if people only had more insight about their behaviors, they could change. Look at these responses:

"Being critical of Jenny's response is just another way of showing you lack understanding."

"Even though you weren't there, out of loyalty to Andy, you insist that he could not have sexually harassed Amy."

"You don't participate in class because you are a shy person and your afraid you will say something that brings attention to you."

"You make fun of this topic because you know some of it applies to you and you're nervous about having someone recognize that."

"You think sexual harassment is funny because that's what you were taught while you were growing up."

An interpretation may be accurate, but most of the time it is only a guess....

The intent is to explain the reason behind the student's thoughts or behavior in the hope that this will provide insight. These responses are marked with "because" terminology and suggest what the student might or should think. There is an attempt to provide some meaning to a situation, but most people do not like to have their behavior or ideas interpreted.

An interpretation may be accurate, but most of the time it is only a guess—a hypothesis at best. Too often interpretative statements are textbook cliches (e.g., "You want other students to laugh at you because you want all the attention.") This may or may not be true, but is it facilitative? Interpretations tend to discourage self-disclosure by confronting people, who then become defensive and hesitate to share their thoughts.

Reassuring

Reassuring responses are intended to tell people we believe in them. These responses are meant as encouragement, but they can easily dismiss someone's feelings and fail to facilitate group discussion. For example:

"That happens to everybody. You know how it is. Boys will be boys."

"Things will turn out okay."

"Your situation reminds me of another girl, Amanda, and she worked things out. You can too."

"It looks bad now, but things will be better tomorrow."

Unfortunately, most of the time reassuring statements miss their

Russell A. Sabella, Ph.D. & Robert D. Myrick, Ph.D.

mark, probably because they imply that individuals need not feel as they do. They suggest one's feelings are common, normal, or temporary. They are often followed by advice, or advice is implied. They suggest one should not be concerned and should feel differently.

Because many facilitators want to push too many things in a single session, they have a tendency to use too many low facilitative responses. Impatience and a press for time often cause facilitators to rush in with low facilitative responses. Low facilitative responses have their place in counseling and guidance activities. You are going to give advice occasionally. You will give reassuring statements, and occasionally you may make interpretations. But, it is timely advice, timely interpretations, and timely reassurance that makes the critical difference.

Facilitative Feedback: Complimenting and Confronting

Feedback, as a process, involves reducing blind areas in a relationship such as when a friend observes you engaging in some type of behavior of which you are unaware. During feedback you are telling another person the impact that person is having on you. The response is a personal one where you express your own feelings that result from being in the presence of that person's behavior.

Students want feedback. They want to know how they are coming across to others. While they may be skeptical of flattering statements or leery of criticisms, they nevertheless are curious about how others experience them and the impressions they make. How can you give students feedback without judging them? How can you compliment or confront students without making them feel defensive?

Students want feedback. They want to know how they are coming across to others.

Facilitative feedback consists of a three part response. It can be either a compliment or a confrontation, depending upon the feelings you want to communicate.

Part 1: Be specific about the behavior. What has the person done? Given an example and be descriptive.

Part 2: Tell how the person's behavior makes you feel. Is your experience a pleasant or unpleasant one? Or both?

Part 3: Tell what your feelings make you want to do. Being in the presence of the person's behavior and feeling as you do, how do you want to respond?

Feedback keeps a focus on the students and, at the same time, discloses some things about yourself. It is an honest response that can be presented in an organized manner so your message is clear. Following are three examples of feedback given to students during one of the sessions about sexual harassment. The first two are compliments and the last is a confrontation. Notice the compliments express pleasant feelings and the confrontation expresses an unpleasant feeling.

"Joseph, you told about a time when you were involved in harassment. You're embarrassed and it wasn't easy, but I appreciate your willingness to explore the issue. Thanks."

"Glennetta, I'm impressed and proud of you. Please keep up the good work. I noticed you kept your small group on task while discussing the sexual harassment scenarios."

"Pat, I am disappointed that you laughed at our example concerning sexual harassment. Your laughter made me uncomfortable and some others too. I can't help but wonder what it was that made you laugh."

In the first example, a compliment was paid to Joseph and the three parts of facilitative feedback were presented in the order of parts 1, 2, and 3. In the case of Glennetta, however, the parts appear in a different order (2, 3, and 1). The order of the feedback parts in a statement is not particularly important, unless their placement may create a different emphasis. In fact, the order of the parts can easily be mixed. Sometimes only the first two parts are relied upon to provide a basic feedback response.

The difference between a compliment and a gentle confrontation can be found in part two, regardless of where it appears in the feedback statement. Your pleasant feelings will be perceived as a compliment, while your unpleasant feelings will probably be viewed as confrontation.

Students will particularly like to hear how they have affected you in a pleasant way. They will enjoy hearing your compliments. It creates warm feelings for them and they will be drawn to you, although first they may feel a little uneasy to hear positive things about themselves. You can help others feel important by tuning into some of the pleasant feelings you experience when they do certain things.

On the other hand, we have learned when we share our unpleasant feelings, there is a tendency for students to be defensive. They may initially pull back and take a second look at you, then probably at themselves. Therefore, there are three guidelines that may be helpful when confronting.

First, do you have any "chips in the bank?" This is another way of asking, "Have you taken the time to listen to the person?" Have you tried to be understanding? Every time that you are an attentive listener and consider the person's feelings, you are putting some "chips in the bank." In essence, you are building up a reserve that can be drawn upon when it is time to confront. Some leaders of the sexual harassment unit have reported they intended to confront students, but after listening to their stories or comments, and after making an effort to discuss their feelings, there was more understanding and less unpleasant feelings. There was no need to confront.

> **Students will particularly like to hear how they have affected you in a pleasant way.**

Timely confrontations are valuable and have a place in a facilitative relationship.

Secondly, is your unpleasant feeling a persistent one? Nobody likes a grouch or someone who "goes off" at every little turn. Life is full of conflict and you do not want to confront everyone who has created some unpleasant feelings in you. When discussing an uncomfortable topic or something that might make you nervous such as sexual harassment, it is natural to exhibit some "nervous laughter." The facilitator must differentiate which is harmless coping and which is ignorant or malicious foolishness. Group feedback may be appropriate and effective in such a case. For example you might say, "I am understanding if sometimes you might feel nervous and giggle a little. I hope that as you become more and more comfortable, that won't happen as much." Timely confrontations are valuable and have a place in a facilitative relationship.

Finally, which words best communicate your ideas? If you are too intense and choose words that are loaded with heavy emotion you run the risk of not being heard. The impact of the feedback response could be diminished, if not dismissed. There are many words which describe unpleasant feelings and could be used in a confrontation with students during a session. Some are similar but have a slightly different shade of meaning.

For instance, it may not be helpful to tell students how much "hate" you feel. It might be better to tell how you feel "irritated" or "annoyed." For example, you might give feedback that goes like this, "Selina, I have watched you argue with your Tic-Tac-Know team on almost every question and now you are arguing with me. I am irritated and suggest that you might listen more." In this example, if the facilitator would have said, "Selina, you argue with your Tic-Tac-Know team on every question. I really hate that and suggest that you listen to them more and help make a team decision." In the latter example, the facilitator may have been too intense and missed the target. Obviously, your choice of words depends upon the situation, your judgment, and your own personal style.

Notice in the example of Selina, the facilitator offers a suggestion. Suggestions or advice, if any, may be included as one aspect of the third part of the feedback model, but it is qualified. It is also lined to the source—your feelings. Those who receive feedback are ultimately responsible for whether they want to continue or to change their behavior. But, they need to know how their behaviors affect others. It is part of the facilitative processes.

Facilitative feedback, whether a compliment or confrontation, is systematic. It offers degree of control over your own emotions. It can generate energy and release tension. After you give feedback to students, it is time to carefully focus your attention on them and tune into any reactions. It is time to continue making facilitative responses to enhance the relationship.

Simple Acknowledgment

Students like to be acknowledged for their contributions. They might be embarrassed or feel awkward if what they say is ignored. Therefore, a simple acknowledgment can be facilitative, especially in a group. A few common simple acknowledgments are:

"Thank you for sharing that."

"Okay."

"Thanks."

"All right."

These responses—and others like them—help avoid the "plop experience"—when someone says something and nobody responds before moving onto something else. It is easy enough to recognize that you heard the person without discussing or making reference to any specific ideas. In addition, such a response is effective in bringing closure to someone's comments or even to a session. It acknowledges but does not encourage the person to talk more—at that time. It is a polite way of telling a person you are now going to move on to another topic or another person.

...such a response is effective in bringing closure to someone's comments....

Linking

The linking response is especially facilitative in groups. Although it could be used to refer to another person who is not present, it is effective when a group leader or facilitator identifies similarities (and perhaps differences) that are occurring among group members. For example:

"Juan, Debbie, and Larry, although somewhat different, you all have had friends who have been harassed, just as we talked about." (Linking content).

"Also, Juan, Debbie, and Larry, as you described your friend's problems, you all felt helpless because you were not sure what to do." (Linking feelings).

As a facilitator, you can look for opportunities to "link" events, ideas, or general experiences students have in common. On the other hand, you can also link feelings. You listen for unpleasant and pleasant feelings as they are being expressed by group members and, on occasion, try to show how these feelings are shared. Following is an example of how a facilitator linked differences between to students:

...similarities that are occurring among group members.

"We are talking about how some people have filed lawsuits involving school boards who have neglected their claims of sexual harassment. Susan, you agree wholeheartedly and think this will force them to analyze their policy against sexual harassment. Al, you, on the other hand, believe these lawsuits add to the frivolous suits that many people are pursuing and winning."

Linking responses help develop a sense of togetherness in a group and add to group cohesiveness. They accentuate relationships by linking information or feelings from one person to another. They enhance the facilitative conditions within a group and, therefore, are listed as one of the six facilitative responses.

Facilitative Responses in Conducting the Unit

The six high facilitative responses described in this chapter are effective with students when you are meeting them individually or leading them in a group discussion. For instance, you may notice a group member is apparently fatigued and struggling to be attentive or participate in the activities. You might make a feeling-focused response such as, "Jimmy, you're tired and it's not easy to be a part of the group right now." Or, if the group is experiencing fatigue, you might say, "As I look around I'm sensing that there is a loss of energy in the group. It seems like we've hit a snag and it's dragging us down."

Likewise, it is possible to clarify a group member's point of view, or some of the ideas that have been expressed by the total group could be summarized. For example, "If I followed you, Angela, you think that our school policy on sexual harassment should be changed." Or, "Let's see now, in the past half hour our group has suggested at least four different ways of changing the policy. First, you said...."

Questions can be directed to an individual or to the total group. Simple acknowledgments are usually made to individuals, but could be directed to the whole group. Linking events and feelings tends to be used in the "here and now" as a group works together.

Group members need to talk with one another, not just to the facilitator.

Compliments can be paid to an individual in a group or to the total group. For instance, "I was pleased and encouraged to see we could start our group on time today, especially knowing we always have so much to cover. It makes me want to make the most of our time together today." Another example might be, "Mark, I was impressed with the way you told us about your situation. You shared some personal information and you were not afraid to talk about your feelings. I'm touched by your courage and trust in us, and I want to honor that trust and confidence."

When a facilitator makes all the responses after each group member has shared something, the process tends to look more like individual counseling before an audience. It chokes off communication among group members—the very strength of the group. Group members need to talk with one another, not just to the facilitator. Therefore, the facilitator should make facilitative responses intermittently among the group members. Further, eliciting the six high facilitative responses from members of the group makes them more responsive to each other. It enhances the facilitative relationship in the group and builds greater cohesiveness.

For instance, you might elicit a feeling-focused response by saying something like this, "Amy's been telling us about some things that are important to her. Let me ask the rest of you in the group, are you hearing pleasant or unpleasant feelings as she talks?" Then, using a "go-around" procedure, several members tell the feelings they heard.

The same might be done with a clarifying or summarizing response. "What basic ideas have we discussed so far today?" Or, "Who can summarize what you heard Jessie say?" Likewise, questions can be elicited. "Who can ask Jessie a question that will help us think some more about what she's been telling us?" "What's a question that needs to be asked at this point?"

You can also elicit a linking response by asking the group to take note of similarities among members. For example, "Who in our group knows someone who has been sexually harassed?" Or, "It seems some of you have had some similar experiences or feelings about sexual harassment. Who remembers the feelings some of our group members shared in common?" Thus, you can respond to individuals within a group or to the group as a whole. You can make the facilitative responses or you can elicit them from group members. Consequently, the original six facilitative responses can be doubled when practiced in groups.

The facilitative responses are not a panacea by themselves.

The facilitative responses are not a panacea by themselves. Taken out of context, they may even appear contrived or phony to you. However, in the context of a guidance unit such as *Confronting Sexual Harassment*, and when used in a timely manner, can be comforting. And, within those relationships, they also help create the facilitative conditions of self-disclosure, feedback, and decision making. They help you accomplish the goals of the guidance unit.

Russell A. Sabella, Ph.D. & Robert D. Myrick, Ph.D.

The Facilitative Activities

The facilitative *responses* are powerful tools and may be adequate alone to facilitate your students. In this guidance unit, for instance, students might be invited to share their knowledge and experiences with sexual harassment, followed by an open discussion of matters. You hope there will be a spontaneous flow of ideas and feelings, as you and your students move toward some guidance objectives. The movement and direction of the group, in this instance, might depend entirely on the dialogue that happens between you and your students.

...facilitative activities can also be used to build relationships and expedite the facilitative processes.

However, facilitative *activities* can also be used to build relationships and expedite the facilitative processes. These activities are considered structured learning experiences, which may be used with individuals or groups. Some activities, like the ones included in this unit for example, are designed to elicit self-disclosure and increase self-awareness. Others encourage self-assessment and feedback. Still others focus on decision-making and problem solving.

The word "activity" is often used to generally describe a planned structured experience. Each activity has a set of "procedures" which outline the steps to be followed. Counselors pay particular attention to procedures since they structure the flow of the session. In addition, participants in an activity are given "tasks" which call for their responses. Some counselors use these terms interchangeably, but it can be useful if they are viewed in more precise terms.

Facilitative *activities* are structured learning experiences which tend to elicit the facilitative process of self-disclosure, feedback, increased awareness and decision making, and responsible action. Some counselors and teachers think of them as exercises. An activity might also be viewed as a composite strategy with procedures and tasks. Facilitative *procedures* are the sequence of steps to be followed. They describe a course of action or a way of doing something. They are the general guidelines which outline a manner of proceeding in a structured experience.

Facilitative *tasks* are specific assignments which direct a person to do something. They may be given alone or as part of some group procedures. One task might request a person to "tell one thing that you could do to reduce the risk of sexual harassment at our school." Another might be "tell one thing that you already do to reduce the risk of sexual harassment from happening around you." These tasks focus on self-disclosure. A person might also be directed to "tell something positive that you have noticed in our group today." Another might be "tell one way that someone impressed you by what they said." Both tasks focus on feedback.

The activities are designed to elicit behaviors and responses from students.

As you might imagine, tasks can also be directed toward decision making or problem solving. For example, "List ten things that our school can do to discourage sexual harassment." Or, "List three pieces of advice that you would give to new students about preventing sexual harassment."

The activities included in *Confronting Sexual Harassment* are organized in a sequence as part of a unit. They are arranged so each session is likely to lead students sequentially through the facilitative processes. Self-disclosure which reflects knowledge and attitude is the first step. After several activities along these lines, it is assumed that students are more open to exploring and making decisions about their own behaviors and the behaviors of others. The activities are designed to elicit behaviors and responses from students. They will help focus a discussion and keep individuals on task. They expedite matters; however, they do not do the work of the facilitator.

After giving students a task, the facilitator must still move them towards their goals. The activities will fail or only show marginal success without your selected use of high facilitative responses to "process" the experience that results from, and during, the activity.

Russell A. Sabella, Ph.D. & Robert D. Myrick, Ph.D.

Accountability and Evaluation

The eventual question is: Did the guidance unit make a positive difference?

The introduction of a unit about sexual harassment to teenagers in schools or agencies requires an awareness that there is a need to help them know more about this social issue. After the need is established, several organizational questions might be asked: Who should be the participants? Should it be a mixed group of boys and girls? Should different grade levels be represented, or should the unit be administered to students in the same age group or class? Who should deliver the unit, peers or adults?

Clearly, the structure and basic procedures that help organize a group of participants to receive the guidance unit, and any supplemental activities, can affect the outcomes. The eventual question is: Did the guidance unit make a positive difference?

The guidance unit in this book directed attention to increased awareness of the problem, knowledge, skills, and attitudes. How are these to be measured? The ultimate objective is that the unit would improve the learning climate in a school and the interpersonal relationships between people.

One way to look at possible outcomes is to use the traditional paper-pencil procedures, where respondents indicate their agreement or disagreement with certain items on an inventory or instrument. A review of the professional literature shows there is a lack of available instruments in this area. There are no known assessment tools that address variables related to sexual harassment sensitivity training such as behavior, attitude, knowledge, and prevalence for middle and high school populations. Instruments that do address sexual harassment have been designed for use within the workplace (e.g., Lee & Heppner, 1991).

Assessing Proclivity for Sexual Harassment

The Sexual Harassment Inventory (SHI) was designed to measure outcomes related to the guidance unit. It consists of 25 items that represent the areas of behavior, attitude, and knowledge about sexual harassment. Respondents read an item and indicate their level of agreement by circling the appropriate response on a Likert-type scale (Strongly Disagree, Disagree, Uncertain, Agree, and Strongly Agree).

The inventory may be administered to an individual or a group. It results in a total score (Proclivity Toward Sexual Harassment) and three sub-scores (Behavior, Attitude, and Knowledge). Several items were generated through a review of the professional literature. These were given to graduate students and professors in psychology and counselor education, who in turn indicated those which appeared to have the most validity. The items were then piloted with approximately 250 middle school students, helping establish both reliability and validity (Sabella, 1995). The instrument is seen in Figure 8.1.

Assessing School Atmosphere

The incidence and prevalence of sexual harassment can make a negative impact upon students' perceived level of comfort in a school. Therefore, decreasing the occurrence of sexual harassment while enhancing effective procedures for handling it when it does occur can contribute to a safe and secure working environment. Included in this chapter is an inventory called The School Atmosphere Inventory (SAI) and may be seen in Figure 8.2. It is provided for you to help assess the unit's impact on overall perception of school comfort. Also, the inventory can be used to collect longitudinal data to assess the long-term effects of the unit on school atmosphere.

Evaluating the Intervention

In addition to the SHI and SAI, you may be interested in knowing what participants thought of the unit. In this case, items are both objective and subjective. Objective items are those that produce results which can be compared between individuals within a group and among individuals between groups. Subjective items may also be compared in this way although they are more meaningful when analyzed individually. Responses to subjective items are not restricted to certain choices. They allow the respondent to provide open answers and insights about the question. Also provided as an assessment tool is a brief survey for this purpose called the Sexual Harassment Unit Evaluation (SHUE), which may be found in Figure 8.3.

Figure 8.1

The Sexual Harassment Inventory
(Sabella & Myrick, 1995)

Age _____ Grade _____ Race _____ Gender _____

School _____ Date_____

For the items below, circle a response that indicates your level of agreement with each statement.

Strongly Disagree (SD)	Agree (A)
Disagree (D)	
	Strongly Agree (SA)
Uncertain (U)	

Sexual Harassment Behavior

SD   D   U   A   SA   1. If I were sexually harassed, I would want to tell a counselor.

SD   D   U   A   SA   2. I am able to say "No" when I mean "No."

SD   D   U   A   SA   3. I am able to report a problem to a teacher when it happens.

SD   D   U   A   SA   4. I know how to report a case of sexual harassment.

SD   D   U   A   SA   5. If I were sexually harassed, I would want to tell a parent.

SD   D   U   A   SA   6. I could help a friend who was sexually harassed.

SD   D   U   A   SA   7. If I were sexually harassed, I would want to tell a friend.

Sexual Harassment Attitudes

SD   D   U   A   SA   8. Even if people dress in a "sexy" way, they do not deserve to be sexually harassed.

SD   D   U   A   SA   9. Nobody likes to be sexually harassed.

SD   D   U   A   SA   10. People who are sexually harassed do not ask for it.

SD   D   U   A   SA   11. When girls say they don't want sexual attention, that is what they really mean.

SD   D   U   A   SA   12. When boys say they don't want sexual attention, they really mean it.

SD   D   U   A   SA   13. A person who is sexually harassed is not relaxed and is not having fun.

Sexual Harassment Knowledge

SD D U A SA 14. I know sexual harassment when I see it.

SD D U A SA 15. Sexual harassment is against school rules.

SD D U A SA 16. Sexual harassment is against the law in the United States.

SD D U A SA 17. If it is difficult to work in school or on a job that lets sexual harassment happen, then it would be a "hostile environment."

SD D U A SA 18. To falsely accuse someone of sexual harassment may put the person in jail or get them fired from a job.

SD D U A SA 19. Sexual harassment can cause emotional pain and suffering.

SD D U A SA 20. Some people think that sexual harassment happens when a person gets excited and cannot control him/herself. This is not true.

SD D U A SA 21. Sexual harassment happens most often in the hallways.

SD D U A SA 22. One of the best ways to deal with sexual harassment is to confront or report it.

SD D U A SA 23. Even if a person was accidently offended by a sexual joke, then it still may be considered sexual harassment.

SD D U A SA 24. There are three main kinds of sexual harassment.

SD D U A SA 25. Sexual harassment happens to about 80% of all middle school students.

Russell A. Sabella, Ph.D. & Robert D. Myrick, Ph.D.

Figure 8.2

The School Atmosphere Inventory

The following questions concern your experiences with your school surroundings. Please be honest and open when answering. Your answers are anonymous and confidential.

Age _____ Grade _____ Race _____ Gender _____

School _____ Date_____

For the items below, circle a response that indicates your level of agreement with each statement.

Strongly Disagree (SD)   Agree (A)

Disagree (D)   Strongly Agree (SA)

Uncertain (U)

SD D U A SA	1. Sexual harassment does not happen often at school.
SD D U A SA	2. I have never been sexually harassed at school.
SD D U A SA	3. I have never seen someone who was being sexually harassed at school.
SD D U A SA	4. I have never sexually harassed someone at school.
SD D U A SA	5. I know what is allowed at school.
SD D U A SA	6. I feel safe at school.
SD D U A SA	7. Teachers at school are helpful.
SD D U A SA	8. I find it easy to talk with school counselors when I meet with them.
SD D U A SA	9. There are no dangerous groups at school.
SD D U A SA	10. My school is a safe place.
SD D U A SA	11. I can feel free to walk anywhere at school without other students giving me trouble.

Figure 8.3

Sexual Harassment Unit Evaluation

The following questions concern your experiences with the sexual harassment activities. Please be honest and open when answering. Your answers are anonymous and confidential.

Age _____ Grade _____ Race _____ Gender _____

School _____ Date _____

For the items below, circle a response that indicates your level of agreement with each statement.

Strongly Disagree (SD)	Agree (A)
Disagree (D)	Strongly Agree (SA)
Uncertain (U)	

SD   D   U   A   SA   1. The sexual harassment unit increased my understanding of others.

SD   D   U   A   SA   2. The unit had an overall positive affect on me.

SD   D   U   A   SA   3. The unit positively affected my behavior towards others.

SD   D   U   A   SA   4. I liked being a member of the group doing the unit.

SD   D   U   A   SA   5. The unit increased understanding of myself.

SD   D   U   A   SA   6. I would recommend the sexual harassment unit experience for others.

SD   D   U   A   SA   7. The unit helped our school to be a better place.

SD   D   U   A   SA   8. This unit helps boys and girls better communicate.

SD   D   U   A   SA   9. I better understand sexual harassment.

SD   D   U   A   SA   10. I have talked to a friend about what I have learned regarding sexual harassment since the unit began.

What one thing that you enjoyed most about your experiences?

What is one thing that you would change about the unit to make it better?

Any other comments or suggestions:

Russell A. Sabella, Ph.D. & Robert D. Myrick, Ph.D.

Scoring and Interpretation

The objective part of the inventories can be scored by assigning numbers to each of the different levels of agreement:

Strongly Disagree (SD) = 1

Disagree (D) = 2

Uncertain (U) = 3

Agree (A) = 4

Strongly Agree (SA) = 5

Then, averages and percentages for each subsection, and a total score, can be obtained. It is suggested that the inventories be completed with "bubble sheets" or "scantrons" so they may more easily be scanned into a computer and analyzed. Researchers may want to conduct more sophisticated analyses such as analysis of variance, multiple regression, reliability coefficients, and chi square procedures to differentiate among groups.

All items on the (1) Sexual Harassment Inventory, (2) School Atmosphere Inventory, and (3) Sexual Harassment Unit Evaluation were written in a consistently positive direction. That means that a high score on each item is desirable.

Sexual Harassment Inventory. The total score on the SHI indicates general proclivity to sexually harass others. Proclivity is the inclination or propensity to sexually harass others. The lower the score, the higher the sexual harassment proclivity. This score can especially be used for screening purposes.

There are three subsections, each of which can be scored separately: Behavior, Attitude, and Knowledge. Behavior deals with actions that are often involved in sexual harassment. Attitude focuses on perceptions, opinions, and outlook related to sexual harassment. Knowledge refers to an awareness and understanding of facts and general information related to the problem of sexual harassment. High score on any and all of these subsections indicates factors which are conducive to mutually respectful and healthy relationships.

What Students Think of the Unit

The activities in this book were conducted with approximately 300 middle school students in Gainesville, Florida. After the unit was completed, students were given the Sexual Harassment Unit Evaluation. Following are the questions and resulting percentages of levels of agreement:

SD = Strongly Disagree
D = Disagree
U = Uncertain
A = Agree
SA = Strongly Agree

Item	SD	D	U	A	SA
1. The sexual harassment unit increased my	6	11	12	50	21
2. The unit had an overall positive	5	11	18	34	32
3. The unit positively affected my behavior	14	29	25	28	4
4. I liked being a member of the group doing the	7	8	20	36	30
5. The unit increased my understanding of	8	23	25	34	11
6. I would recommend the sexual harassment unit	8	17	15	40	20
7. The unit helped our school to be a better	18	24	42	11	5
8. This unit helps boys and girls better	7	19	32	34	8
9. I better understand sexual harassment	8	8	13	46	25
10. I have talked to a friend about what I	27	31	12	19	11

The percentage of students who agree that they better understand sexual harassment was approximately 71%. Also, 71% of participants reported that they increased their understanding of others. Sixty-six percent of students experiencing the unit reported that it had a positive impact on them. Students who participated in the guidance unit about sexual harassment reported that they had a worthwhile and enjoyable learning experience that helped them to advance their understanding of the nature of sexual harassment.

Russell A. Sabella, Ph.D. & Robert D. Myrick, Ph.D.

What Students Said

Students wrote about their ideas and feelings about the unit. Presented now is representative sample of those comments expressed by middle school students after completing the unit. The unit was facilitated both by counselors and trained high school peer facilitators.

"I had lots of fun doing the unit...."

"I like that we could talk in class...."

"I think it's great that you and the teachers are teaching us this, because we need to know how to deal with sexual harassment."

"I think I learned a lot because when I was in fourth grade my friend got harassed and I didn't know what to do but now I do. I learned a lot this year."

"I enjoyed just being able to talk about it."

"The activities taught me a lot and they were fun.... It gives you a lot of facts and keeps you interested with activities."

"There was a lot of stuff I learned that I did not know of."

"... I thought it was a fun way to learn about sexual harassment. It was fun doing it and watching other people."

"I·really wanted to do more activities. I wanted to learn more about this."

"I liked it when we had to answer questions about the scenarios and the Four Corners activity too."

"Now I know what to say to a person if they sexually harass me.... You know who to talk to."

"I would make it be taught for fifth graders."

"I enjoyed learning the facts about sexual harassment. I would have more lessons."

"I think you did a good job on making it fun and educational."

"I liked the role playing. It puts you in a situation where you would have to know what to say."

"I enjoyed it because it would help you know about it and know if you were getting sexually harassed."

"One thing that I liked was they didn't make it boring.... I learned a lot of stuff about SH like what to do when you are put in the situation. The peer counselors did a very good job especially with the games."

"We got to learn about something we knew very little about. We learned what sexual harassment is. I think the unit should go into more detail."

Both student ratings and written comments about the unit help facilitators know how to properly tailor a unit for their specific population. With student feedback, facilitators and other school personnel can be assured that their sexual harassment intervention efforts are working. Specifically, positive student feedback can help facilitators to feel confident about achieving the goals they have established. Negative feedback is also useful for knowing exactly how to alter the format of your unit so you can better meet the special needs of your class or school.

Session
Reproducibles

Russell A. Sabella, Ph.D. & Robert D. Myrick, Ph.D.

Session 1: Reproducible

Strongly Disagree

Russell A. Sabella, Ph.D. & Robert D. Myrick, Ph.D.

Uncertain

Russell A. Sabella, Ph.D. & Robert D. Myrick, Ph.D.

Agree

Strongly Agree

Scenario 1

Brian and Joe, both in the same English class, make comments about what type of girls they like. One day Brian says to Joe, "I like `em with little round butts." Brian laughed as usual. Jill was a girl in the next row and heard the comments. She told them that she found such talk disgusting and asked them to stop. Both Brian and Joe apologized to Jill. The next day, Jill once again overheard Brian in a deliberately loud voice make a similar comment. Brian and Joe continued to ignore Jill's confrontations. Jill began to feel helpless and upset. She found it very difficult to concentrate in class.

1. Is this sexual harassment? Why?

2. What could Jill have done to make it stop?

3. How else might Brian and Joe respond to Jill's complaints?

4. In addition to being offensive to Jill, what else is wrong with comments such as the one Brian and Joe made?

Scenario 2

Carl rides the bus to school and back home every day. Just for fun, he wrote a note to Juanita and passed it to her. The note read, "You have a really nice body. How about you and I get together? Come over tonight!." After Juanita read the note and looked up at Carl, he made some sexual gestures with his hands, eyebrows, and lips.

1. Is this sexual harassment? Why?

2. How might Juanita have felt if Carl's behavior was unwanted?

3. Why might Carl have acted this way?

Russell A. Sabella, Ph.D. & Robert D. Myrick, Ph.D.

Scenario 3

A group of four girls frequently whistle "wolf calls" at Jamal. Jamal thought it was kind of neat and enjoyed the special attention. After a while, when the girls didn't stop, Jamal began to feel embarrassed and uncomfortable. He no longer considered the attention special and began to feel upset. He told them to quit but they would laugh and continue. Jamal didn't really know what to do. Jamal just wanted to be left alone.

1. Is this sexual harassment? Why?

2. Do boys really experience sexual harassment?

3. What might the girls have thought about Jamal's request for them to stop whistling at him? Why?

4. What might some of the other boys think if they knew that Jamal told the girls to stop whistling?

Session 5: Reproducible—You Gizzydeech Cards

Read with excitement:
"You are such a *GIZZYDEECH*.

Read with NO feeling:
"You are such a *GIZZYDEECH*.

Read with sadness:
"You are such a *GIZZYDEECH*.

Read with surprise:
"You are such a *GIZZYDEECH*.

Read with anger:
"You are such a *GIZZYDEECH*.

Read with depression:
"You are such a *GIZZYDEECH*.

Read with pride:
"You are such a *GIZZYDEECH*.

Read with confusion:
"You are such a *GIZZYDEECH*.

Read with fear:
"You are such a *GIZZYDEECH*.

Read with love:
"You are such a *GIZZYDEECH*.

Russell A. Sabella, Ph.D. & Robert D. Myrick, Ph.D.

Session 5: Reproducible—The Blind Spot Paragraph

One of the best feelings is the feeling of love. If a person is a friend of yours, and you love them, that is also a special kind of love. Feelings of fear sometimes come with love.

One of the best feelings is the feeling of love. If a person is a friend of yours, and you love them, that is also a special kind of love. Feelings of fear sometimes come with love.

One of the best feelings is the feeling of love. If a person is a friend of yours, and you love them, that is also a special kind of love. Feelings of fear sometimes come with love.

One of the best feelings is the feeling of love. If a person is a friend of yours, and you love them, that is also a special kind of love. Feelings of fear sometimes come with love.

One of the best feelings is the feeling of love. If a person is a friend of yours, and you love them, that is also a special kind of love. Feelings of fear sometimes come with love.

Session 6: Reproducibles—Party Game Labels

Cut these sheets and tape one to each student's back without that person seeing it. Randomly choose students balanced for gender and race.

Disregard the topic and make comments about my feet! Say things like, "Ooooh, those are the best looking pair of feet I have ever seen!"

I might be interested in going together with you.

I hate it when people look me directly in the eyes when talking with me.

Russell A. Sabella, Ph.D. & Robert D. Myrick, Ph.D.

Session 6: Reproducibles—Party Game Labels

Cut these sheets and tape one to each student's back without that person seeing it. Randomly choose students balanced for gender and race.

I like to talk with others ONLY when there is nobody around. You can't talk with me until we are alone.

I like people to get up close to me when I'm talking with them. Stand about two feet away.

You are extremely interested in what I have to say.

Session 6: Reproducibles—Party Game Labels

Cut these sheets and tape one to each student's back without that person seeing it. Randomly choose students balanced for gender and race.

I scare you. Act nervous when talking to me.

I am not comfortable with people "in my face." Stay at least five feet away when talking to me.

You find me physically attractive.

Russell A. Sabella, Ph.D. & Robert D. Myrick, Ph.D.

Cut these sheets and tape one to each student's back without that person seeing it. Randomly choose students balanced for gender and race.

You are VERY interested in getting my phone number. You don't want to leave without it.

Disregard the topic and make comments about my hands! Say things like, "Ooooh, those are the best looking pair of hands I have ever seen!"

I like to hold hands when I'm talking to a friend.

Helping a Friend Who Has Been Sexually Harassed

You Can...

- Lend a listening ear.
- Go with your friend to get help.
- Have patience if your friend does not "get over it" as quickly as you would like.
- Continue your efforts to understand even when it gets confusing.
- Help confront the perpetrator.
- Ask, "What can I do to help you?"

You Should Not...

- Blame your friend in any way for the sexual harassment.
- Dismiss the act as "no big deal."
- Laugh or make light of the situation.
- Give advice or make decisions for your friend.
- Ignore your friend's situation.
- Gossip about the situation to others.

Resource Telephone Numbers

Police Department _____

Sheriff's Organization _____

Crisis Intervention Center _____

School Resource Officer _____

Others _____

_____

_____

Russell A. Sabella, Ph.D. & Robert D. Myrick, Ph.D.

Session 7: Reproducible

Options for Confronting Sexual Harassment

The following options can be used with people who force unwanted sexual attention on us. You can try any one, more than one, or all of the options.

REMINDER: Write down everything you attempt when trying to make someone stop sexually harassing you. Also, tell your parents/guardians as soon as you feel like you are being sexually harassed.

**Option:
Communicate Your Noncompliance**

Make this straight forward and clear. "STOP ... (the behavior)! Also communicate your feelings, "I am disgusted."

**Option:
Confront the Person**

Put the focus on the harasser: "What is it about you that makes you continue to sexually harass me? Why is it so important to you? What do you get out of it? You seem to be getting something out of sexually harassing me, what is it? One more time: *No!*

**Option:
Make an Unofficial Complaint**

Tell a school official that you trust such as a teacher, counselor, administrator, secretary.

**Option:
Focus on the Consequence**

Tell the consequences of their being persistent. "If you keep sexually harassing me by ..., then I will file an official complaint with our principal and the school resource officer. Sexual harassment is a crime punishable by fines and jail time!"

**Option:
Clarify the Situation**

Clarify what the person is doing: "You are making unwanted sexual comments to me... even though I have told you to stop. That is sexual harassment!

**Option:
Make an Official Complaint**

Use the Memorandum handout to log an official complaint with a school administrator or counselor. Also tell a parent about what has been happening.

Memo

DATE: _____ (Today's Date)

FROM: _____ (Student's Name)

TO: _____ Administrator's Name)

RE: Possible Sexual Harassment

_____

I want to talk with you about an incident that happened on _____. The incident involves:

_____

_____

_____

_____

_____

_____

_____

❏ I confronted this person on _____ (date).

❏ I have NOT confronted this person.

❏ I already told _____.

Signed,

_____

Student

Russell A. Sabella, Ph.D. & Robert D. Myrick, Ph.D.

Session 8: Reproducible Contract

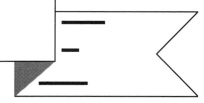

Contract

I, _____,
promise to remain aware of sexually harassing behaviors, gestures, and activities, and to refrain from such behaviors, gestures, and activities. I am committed to *healthy, respectful* relationships with all others. I will, to the best of my ability, confront sexually harassing activities such as:

- Unwanted communications, notes, letters, or other written materials of a sexual nature.
- Unwanted suggestions, comments, or remarks about a person's clothing, body, or activities of a sexual nature.
- Unwanted suggestive or insulting sounds.
- Unwanted whistling of a suggestive manner.
- Unwanted humor and jokes that puts down others.
- Unwanted sexual propositions, invitations, or pressure for sexual activity.
- Obvious or not-so-obvious sexual threat(s).
- Patting, pinching, or other unwanted touching.
- Unwanted physical exposure.
- Unnecessary and unwanted touching or brushing against the body.
- Attempted or actual kissing or fondling that is not consensual.

Failure to honor this contract can result in physical, emotional, and/or spiritual injury, possible suspension from school, prosecution, and/or incarceration. I realize that I can report sexual harassment to a teacher, counselor, administrator, or other adult who I trust.

_____   _____
Student Signature   Facilitator Signature

_____   _____
Date   Date

Certificate
of Completion

_____

is hereby recognized
as successfully completing
a unit entitled
Confronting Sexual Harassment

This _____ day of _____, 199___

_____

Group Facilitator

    Russell A. Sabella, Ph.D. & Robert D. Myrick, Ph.D.

References and Related Readings

Abbey, A. (1982). Sex differences in attributions for friendly behavior: Do males misperceive females' friendliness? *Journal of Personality and Social Psychology, 42,* 830-838.

Bartling, C.A. & Eisenman, R. (1993). Sexual harassment proclivities in men and women. *Bulletin of the Psychonomic Society, 31(3),* 189-192.

Bogart, K., & Stein, N. (1987). Breaking the silence: Sexual harassment in education. *Peabody Journal of Education, 64(4),* 146-163.

Bouchard, E. (1990). *Everything you need to know about sexual harassment.* New York: Rosen Publishing Group.

Burt, M.R. (1991). Rape myths and acquaintance rape. In A. Parrot & L. Bechhofer (Eds.), *Acquaintance rape: The hidden crime* (pp. 26-40). New York: John Wiley & Sons.

Carroll, L., & Ellis, K. L. (1989). Faculty attitudes toward sexual harassment: Survey results, survey process. *Initiatives, 52(3),* 35-42.

Crichton, M. (1993). *Disclosure.* New York: Alfred A. Knopf.

Facts on sexual harassment. (1985). Washington, DC: National Organization of Women Legal Defense and Education Fund.

Feltey, K.M., Ainslie, J.J., & Geib, A. (1991). Sexual coercion attitudes among high school students: The influence of gender and rape education. *Youth & Society, 23(2).*

Gutek, B. (1985). Sex and the workplace: *The impact of sexual behavior and harassment on women, men, and organizations.* New York: Josey-Bass.

Harris, R. (1993). *Hostile hallways: The AAUW survey on sexual harassment in America's schools.* Washington, DC: AAUW Educational Foundation.

Hotelling, K. (1991). Sexual harassment: A problem shielded by silence. *Journal of Counseling & Development, 69(6).*

Howard, S. (1991). Organizational resources for addressing sexual harassment. *Journal of Counseling & Development, 69(6).*

Illinois Task Force on Sexual Harassment and Sangamon State University. (1980). *Task force survey reported to Illinois House Judiciary Committee.* Springfield: Sangamon State University.

Lee, L.A., & Heppner, P.P. (1991). The development and evaluation of a sexual harassment inventory. *Journal of Counseling & Development, 69(6).*

LEXIS/NEXIS user's guide. (1993). Center for Instructional and Research Computing Activities, E520 Computer Science and Engineering, University of Florida, Gainesville, FL 32611-2024.

Lumsden, L.S. (1992). *Getting serious about sexual harassment.* (ERIC Document Reproduction Service No. ED 347 699).

McCaghy, M.D. (1985). *Sexual harassment.* Boston: G.K. Hall & Company.

McKinney, K., & Maroules, N. (1991). *Sexual harassment.* Lexington, MA: Lexington Books.

Morris, B., Terpstra, J., Croninger, B., & Linn, E. (1985). *Tune in to your rights: A guide for teenagers about turning off sexual harassment.* Ann Arbor: The University of Michigan.

Myrick, R.D., & Sorenson, D.L. (1992). *Teaching helping skills to middle school students: Program leaders guide.* Minneapolis, MN: Educational Media Corporation.

Myrick, R.D., & Myrick, L.S. (1990). *The teacher advisor program: An innovative approach to school guidance.* Ann Arbor, MI: ERIC/CAPS.

Myrick, R.D. (1993). *Developmental guidance and counseling: A practical approach* (2nd ed.). Minneapolis, MN: Educational Media Corporation.

Myrick, R.D., & Folk, B.E. (1991). *The power of peervention: A manual for the trainers of peer facilitators.* Minneapolis, MN: Educational Media Corporation.

Petrocelli, W., & Repa, B.K. (1992). *Sexual harassment on the job: What it is and how to stop it.* Berkeley, CA: Nolo Press.

Powell, G.N. (1986). Effects of sex role identity and sex on definitions of sexual harassment. *Sex Roles, 14(1-2),* 9-19.

Pryor, J. (1987). Sexual harassment proclivities in men. *Sex Roles, 17,* 269-290.

Reilly, L.B., Lott, B., Caldwell, D., & DeLuca, L. (1992). Tolerance for sexual harassment related to self-reported sexual victimization. *Gender & Society, 6(1),* 122-138.

Reilly, L.B. (1992). *Study to examine actions perceived as sexual harassment.* (ERIC Document Reproduction Service No. ED 359 378).

Sabella, R.A. (1995). The effectiveness of a developmental guidance unit and self-instruction module about sexual harassment. Unpublished doctoral dissertation, University of Florida, Gainesville, FL.

Sandler, B.R. (1989). Sexual harassment: A new issue for institutions. *Initiatives, 52(3),* 5-10.

Shoop, R.J., & Edwards, D.L. (1994). *How to stop sexual harassment in our schools: A handbook and curriculum guide for administrators and teachers.* Des Moines, IA: Paramount Publishing.

Stein, N.D. (1991). It happens here too: Sexual harassment in the schools. *Education Week, 32(25).*

Strauss, S. (1988). Sexual harassment in the school: Legal implications for principals. *NASSP Bulletin, 72(506),* 93-97.

Strauss, S. (1992). *Sexual harassment and teens: A program for positive change.* Minneapolis, MN: Free Spirit Publishing.

Tannen, D. (1990). *You just don't understand: Women and men in conversation.* New York: William Morrow.

Terpstra, D.E. (1987). *A hierarchy of sexual harassment. Journal of Psychology, 121(6).*

Thacker, R.A. (1994). Innovative steps to take in sexual harassment prevention. *Business Horizons, 37(1),* 29.

Wellesley College Center for Research on Women. (1992). *The AAUW report: How schools shortchange girls.* Washington, DC: AAUW Educational Foundation.

Woody, R.H. & Perry, N.W. (1993). Sexual harassment victims: Psychological and family therapy considerations. *American Journal of Family Therapy, 21(2),* 136-144.